IMAGES
OF
W.B. YEATS
JAMES JOYCE
FEDERICO GARCIA LORCA
PICASSO
SAMUEL BECKETT
FRANCIS BACON
1975 — 1987

LOUIS LE BROCQUY

ISBN 0-906627-18-4
PUBLISHED BY THE ARTS COUNCIL
70 MERRION SQUARE, DUBLIN 2.

COVER: 43 IMAGE OF SAMUEL BECKETT, 1987 (DETAIL)
BACK COVER: 31 IMAGE OF PICASSO, 1983. MUSEE PICASSO, ANTIBES
SEE LIST OF WORKS PP 76-80

This exhibition of paintings by Louis le Brocquy is one of an ongoing series presented on an annual basis by the Arts Council and the Arts Council of Northern Ireland, which is intended to pay tribute to some of our more distinguished Irish artists. Previous artists who have been honoured in this way have included Tony O'Malley and William Scott.

The present exhibition represents a central aspect of le Brocquy's work, being a selection of his head images over the past twelve years.

We are grateful to the Guinness Hop Store, Dublin, and the Ulster Museum, Belfast, for making their galleries available to us for this exhibition. We would also like to welcome the involvement in this exhibition of the Cultural Relations Committee of the Department of Foreign Affairs under whose aegis this exhibition will travel to the National Gallery of Victoria, Melbourne, in 1988 as part of the Australian Bi-centenial celebrations. The Arts Councils would like to thank the lenders who have so generously loaned their works to this exhibition. Special thanks too are extended to the many distinguished writers who have contributed to this publication.

In particular, we would like to thank the artist and his wife Anne Madden for the considerable time and assistance they put into helping with organising the exhibition.

JOHN HUNT
VISUAL ARTS OFFICER
THE ARTS COUNCIL

LOUIS LE BROCQUY'S WITNESSES

And let us, ciphers to this great accompt,
On your imaginary forces work.

SHAKESPEARE, HENRY V

Louis McNeice related in his autobiography that he and E.R. Dodds, that splendid Greek scholar and lively soul, went to tea with W. B. Yeats in Rathfarnham in September 1934. Yeats' manner, writes McNeice, "was hierophantic, even when he said: 'This afternoon I have been playing croquet with my daughter." (...) He talked a great deal about the spirits to whom his wife, being a medium, had introduced him. "Have you ever seen them?" Dodds asked (Dodds could never keep back such questions). Yeats was a little piqued. No, he said grudgingly, he had never actually seen them... but — with a flash of triumph — he had often *smelt* them".

This vignette came back to me the other day as I was looking at Louis le Brocquy's images of Yeats among others. The great prophetic Irish poet has become a hovering spirit himself now, though some of those who have received similar honours from le Brocquy — Samuel Beckett and Francis Bacon among them — are still alive and, we hope, well.

Associations of ideas can sometimes make one wonder, and idle wondering can yield a clue. In the cross currents of what was once known as modernity (and has only recently been tied down to a post), a number of painters have seemed to be involved in the difficult and grimly prophetic task of breaking up the human face until what remained on the canvas was pure vivisected torment in oil. In the best of cases, even as the man's face succumbed, the paint continued to lead its own, independent life, transmuting the current agony to a painful, illuminating delight.

Critics, all too often, sought to rationalise this new and disquieting vision, explaining it away in terms of an endless pursuit of "freedom". But this was a mere formalisation of what was actually going on and the uninformed public was no doubt closer to the truth when it experienced anxiety at the sight of such paintings. This anxiety naturally led to the rejection of the painting, whereas it would have been more appropriate to wonder what more immediate threat the painting might forebode.

Some have sought to account for these images by explaining that they reflected the monstrous violence of our century. I suspect, however, that

[4]

both the images *and* the proliferation of violence were a consequence of something else — of the terrifying prospect which some have referred to as "the disappearance of man" and which Yeats has concisely and once more prophetically expressed in "The Second Coming".

Le Brocquy's heads, no doubt reflect this situation too, but their obstinate, quasi ritual recurrence, their insistent multiplication, together with certain features I would like to talk about now, give them an entirely different significance and place them on the further and, I hope, future slope of our world.

Reaching back to Byzantium we find these fully designated figures — I almost wrote, fully fleshed out, but there is little to suggest flesh in these mosaics — standing out on a wall of gold, facing us, wide eyed, almost facing us *down*, like countless witnesses emerging out of a timeless golden fog and standing at the frontier of their world without space, up there on the wall, to summon us, remind us of our still incomplete humanity.

They stand in something like another element, denser and more easeful than our own, and our own world seems embarrassingly circumstantial when confronted with theirs — just like a child's world may seem full of idiosyncratic whims to an older person who has never had children. The figures are so self-possessed while we ourselves never quite manage to get a grip on ourselves, but constantly elude ourselves and pursue ourselves through all becoming, seeking the single, enigmatic point through which we are anchored in being.

Louis le Brocquy has just now (*) gone down into the vast mediaeval kitchen of the intellect and come up with two peculiar utensils which may give cause to wonder to those of us who are used to the smooth aluminium saucepans of today. In the left hand he carries an object that Tinguely might have designed. It is labelled *Quodditas*. In the right hand he holds its quasi twin, *Quidditas*. Ask him what they are for and he will put their names into modern English: one contains the "That" of things and is known as the "Thatness" — the other holds their "What" and is known as the 'Whatness". But of course, those of us who are not familiar with mediaeval cuisine will not feel so easily enlightened and so I shall try to amplify according to my own lights.

"That" we are, we know well enough. But "what" we are remains in suspense. "Thatness", in this sense, is merely the flush of a formless striving to become. "Whatness", is the mark of being fully achieved. We can say *what* it is. Not so, with ourselves. The figures on the Byzantine wall, however, are all fully defined — their *Quidditas*, their "Whatness" is unfolded, they hold no further surprise or uncertainty. Or again, in Chaplin's City Lights, the tramp is pure "Thatness" while the blind girl, who imagines things in an ideal form, lends him a mistaken "Whatness" — he is to her mind the wealthy and powerful man who allowed her to regain her sight and then disappeared. At the end of course, she sees this pitiful little man suffering pathetic indignities from street urchins, touches his hand when she presses a coin into it, and thereupon recognises him. It is this general discrepancy and passing co-incidence between our "Thatness" and our "Whatness" that caused grown men to sob quite uncontrollably when the film was first released.

It is this discrepancy and this ever sought after coincidence, (viewed here in a contemporary context) which are, I believe, the constant matter of le Brocquy's art. As I suggested earlier, he appears to be seeking the single point through which we are anchored in being. That point is here the human eye — the two eyes (even though half occluded, half-blind at times) that, rising out of these paintings, grasp us, sink into us like fish-hooks. The faces meanwhile appear to take shape quite fortuitously despite — or because of the independent life led by the paint on canvas.

Le Brocquy's own prophecy does not concern the vanishing of man but his extraordinarily tenacious persistency in being. This will to be, to become, to emerge, to assert, finds expression in the eyes which, on the white canvas, compel the random dabs of color to become a face and a declaration of intent.

Almost we do not see them — but we smell them out: we smell out the sweating will, the prophetic pursuit of the poetic witnesses chosen by le Brocquy. They are witnesses not to "man" as an accomplished being, but to the endless striving to find and grasp that enigmatic creature that we ourselves create and seek to be — that Whatness monster that has so often been sighted, though its existence, for obvious reasons, has not yet been proven to the satisfaction of all.

MICHAEL GIBSON
PARIS, 1987

(*) "Just now" is no more than a narrative convenience. The text to which I allude, published in Dorothy Walker's book on Louis le Brocquy, was written in 1979.

FACES OF YEATS

Yeats, the most varied mind of the Irish race, the last — and perhaps the only — Romantic poet in English to manage a full career. Le Brocquy, the most dedicated Irish painter since Yeat's brother died, with an intuitive sympathy for literature and mythology, an increasingly rare reverence before the human.

Their meeting has an aspect of inevitability. In the last decade le Brocquy has reinvented for himself the idea of portraiture, moving through family and friends to contemplate master spirits of his country, like Joyce and Beckett.

As he says "simply because by their works I know them, and am drawn to peer through their familiar, ambiguous faces which mask — and at the same time embody — the great worlds of their vision".

And now Yeats, whom le Brocquy knew as a boy. Fascinatingly, the ideals and techniques of the two artists have much in common. One of the foolishnesses of modern psychology is to believe that we have only a few, usually warring, selves. But a Prospero, like Yeats, may live many lives, inhabit many faces, while achieving a unity in variety. At an early stage, he began to play with his doctrine of the Mask, the anti-self, as a discipline for spiritual or physical plenitude. "I call to my own opposite", he says, "all / That I have least looked upon".

Let us examine his selves, as they pass before us, in slow procession. There is the dreamy young man who pressed himself to the earth of Sligo and Howth, like a lover. He wanted to go and live on an island, or in a cave, like Shelley's Alastor, a young man burdened with dreams.

But dreams can be harnessed and that young romantic, a cowslick of hair carefully plastered over his brow, is a more wily customer that he seems. George Moore might wickedly compare his cawing voice to a crow's, his solemn poet's robes to an umbrella left behind at a picnic, but he also testified to his intellectual strength. It took a masterful man to found and manage the Abbey Theatre, to propagandise for an Irish Literary Renaissance.

So the tuneless crow becomes a sacerdotal heron, a high priest of the arts. And the gaunt celibate becomes a great lover,who kneels before Maud Gonne, the English army captain's daughter who was his personification of Ireland, as Petrarch did before Laura, Homer before Helen. Love has as many allotropes as carbon — from soot to diamond — and Yeats weathered all the stages, crying out in frustration for the bosom of his "faery bride", swearing friendship with Olivia Shakespeare, collaborating with Lady Gregory, achieving a profoundly psychic exchange in his marriage with his medium wife.

For Yeats was a trained mystic, a member of the Order of the Golden Dawn, who did not play with, but actually practised magic. Technically, le Brocquy's method is akin to that of certain noble poems of Yeats where he names and numbers his friends, living and dead, or sets different aspects of himself to dialogue, even to dance. So the painter invokes faces of the poet, public and private, to challange and exchange.

Compare earlier and later visages. The short-sighted sighing inventor of the Celtic Twighlight is now a "smiling public man" (No. 5). The right eye sharp, the left hooded, he exudes a satisfied power, like a replete bird of prey, "the lidless eye that loves the sun". The cowslick becomes a crest, a ruffled plumage, and the wide black riband, falling from the tortoise-shell-rimmed glasses, is set like a bar across his face. Significantly le Brocquy moves towards whiteness, the full majesty of paint, as the poet moves towards wholeness, definition. But with friends, Yeats could still display the full battery of his moods, changing from rage to affection, from solemnity to boyishness, in a single instant, like sun chasing shadow across a West of Ireland field.

For behind the silver-haired Senator, the majestic black hatted Nobel Prize winner, with his carefully rehearsed gestures, is still the young poet, the spiritual fanatic in search of truth. Crow, heron, eagle, scarecrow, le Brocquy dwells with wonder on the changing roles of Yeats; but my supreme favourite amoung these psychic portraits, these attempts to show how the spirit speaks and shines through the casket of the brain, the exposed or retreated eye, the chosen regalia, is one which combines the earlier and later selves (No. 3). The eyes are lifted triumphantly above the glasses, the lips are widening to smile, the hair is in disarray; this man has lived a strenuous life of achievement, has glimpsed truth and is not afraid of death : his "ancient glittering eyes are gay".

JOHN MONTAGUE

Preface to catalogue *Louis le Brocquy. A la Recherche de Yeats*, Musée d'Art Moderne de la Ville de Paris, 1976. Etudes Irlandaises, C.E.R.I.U.L., Lille 1977.

[8]

7
IMAGE OF
W.B. YEATS
1975, (DETAIL)

1 IMAGE OF W.B. YEATS 1975, (DETAIL)

[10]

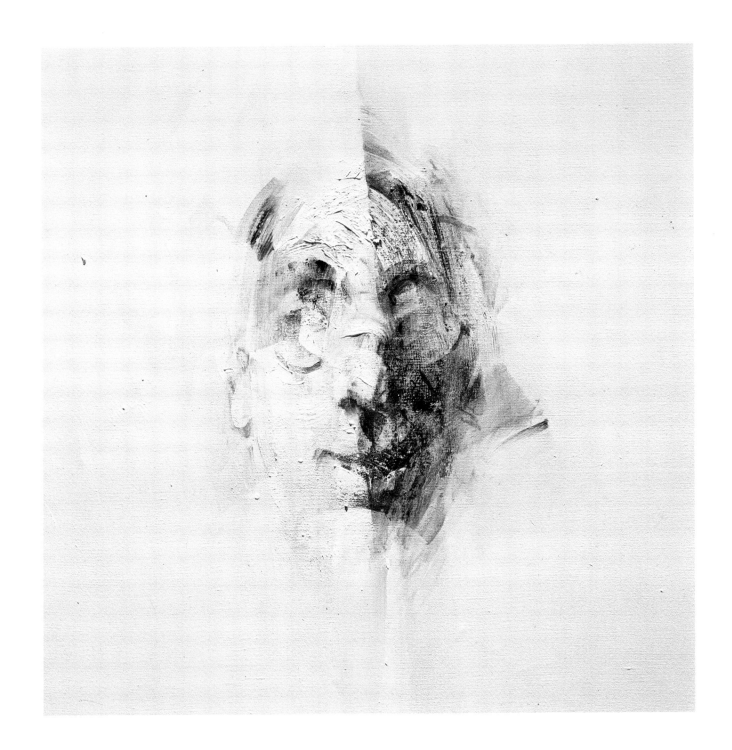

3 IMAGE OF W.B. YEATS 1975, (DETAIL)

8 IMAGE OF W.B. YEATS 1981

[12]

COMMITMENT OF THE IMAGINATION

Interview with Louis le Brocquy by Bernard Noël

Bernard Noël — Your endeavour to create a non-realist portrait, a non-figurative figuration, questions the nature not only of psychological representation, but of the image itself. Francis Bacon defined the nature of the venture with some precision when he wrote: "Louis le Brocquy belongs to a category of artists who have always existed — obsessed by figuration outside and on the other side of illustration — who are aware of the vast and potent possibilities of inventing ways by which fact and appearance can be reconjugated..." The work you show might therefore be considered something of a challenge.

Louis le Brocquy — Indeed I have asked myself whether this series of studies without logic, without end, could mean very much to other people; whether they could perceive at all the interior adventure it represented for me. It started simply enough with a commisssion from a Swedish organisation for an aquatint purporting to pay tribute to a Nobel prize-winner. I chose Yeats, having known him when I was a boy and because of his vast and mysterious personality. I soon realised that a single, definitive portrait was no longer possible. Since the advent of photography, the cinema, psychology, it is no longer credible. So I began to make a succession of studies, referring to numerous photographs, spreading them out before me irrespective of age, trying to discover an image underlying the ever-changing external appearance of the man. I wanted to find a sort of Yeatsiness, an essence of Yeats. Of course I never fully succeeded in this, since it is not possible to evoke the whole of Yeats.

B.N. — The face is an indication which is perhaps rather too insistent. Genius has a name. If this name be given a multiplicity of faces, will it not thus be obliterated?

L. le B. — Yeats is a mountain range, with its peaks and its hollows... I am fascinated by the mutability of faces, of heads. Previously my work was based on the torso — the torso seen as an image of the human being. Some twelve years ago I began to conceive the *head* as an image of the whole in the part. For our Celtic ancestors, I imagine, the head was a box which holds the spirit prisoner but which at the same time manifests this spirit. Paradoxically, the head is simultaneously a mask which hides the mind and a revelation, an incarnation of mind. Painting is not a very good instrument, perhaps, to deal with this kind of thing. One can be accused all too easily of being literary. I search for something of the head without knowing precisely what I am looking for. I don't want to express myself. I try to scuffle the surface of the paper or the canvas, to penetrate the surface rather like an archaeologist in order to see what may emerge. As an archaeologist I cheat, since I know perfectly well beforehand that something lies there outside myself and that I shall cause it to emerge onto the surface... Yeats himself was fascinated by what he called his 'mask', his own antithesis. He tried to bring his 'mask' to the surface of his personality...

B.N. — Are you then trying to realise this "mask" of Yeats? But of course not; Yeats may seem to appear, but in reality it is painting...

L. le B. — To realise something effective in painting I think one must forget about any self-conscious activity and fill oneself with meaning, with curiosity. Sometimes in this way one can perhaps achieve beauty, whereas if beauty is attempted directly, only prettiness can result. One must forget...

B.N. — Forget Yeats in order to paint Yeats?

L. le B. — Yes, in a subjective sense I have tried to do just that. Since the Renaissance it has been generally believed that what is exterior is real. Reality was equated with exterior phenomena; but during long periods it was thought that reality was to be found within the mind, the spirit. Our spirit is a transformer. The hand can act as an independent being to bring about the emergence of an image; one waits for this without imposing oneself, watching for what may happen. I am convinced that Paleolithic man acted in this way. He was an artist, but above all a seer. There is a brain in the hand. The hand in the grotto of Pech-Merle is a personality. A hand-print is a personality. A footprint is only a trace, an imprint. Why?... When I am working I do not think other than in a narrow, technical sort of way. Painting is a form of thought within which a wider, personal intelligence plays no immediate part. It has its own logic. For me, at any rate, there is no question of invention; one can only hope for discovery. Invention for me is recognition. When I am painting, marks combine to form *objets trouvés* which may be recognised. One tries to preserve these and to induce something further. If that works, an entire image may emerge. If not, it will fail. In this particular work Yeats was my Virgil, my guide in this Hades. He gave me stability, reference. Wherever I strayed, trying to find his image, to make it palpable, he held me on his trail. At times I even had the feeling of touching him. At times I was a charlatan who toyed with the apparition of Yeats, as one might struggle to conjure up the dead in spiritualism. In my work struggle, fatigue is a very important element. An image seldom emerges from the canvas, it seems, without tiredness — a tiredness at times to the point of despair, failure, humiliation. Those who can find the strength to continue in face of this may sometimes succeed... It is an interior struggle involving oneself. In this sense perhaps the canvas is the surface of a mirror.

B. N. — Then Yeats, the face of Yeats, is for you a sort of alibi?

L. le B. — Yes, but I don't care to admit it consciously. The hand can lead us away from ourselves and discover the "mask". But what hides also reveals... An artist tends to paint his self-portrait all the time, since what he tries to draw up from the depths of the paper, or the canvas, lies really somewhere in his own head. Such intimate knowledge as one has of another human being through his works — yes, all that one knows of him — passes behind this billowing curtain, the face. And if this curtain be carefully drawn aside, one is liable sometimes to find only poor traces of oneself. I imagine that Rembrandt displayed the highest intelligence in projecting conscious ideas of himself into his self-portraits. In this sense they are not really self-portraits, but rather portraits of a man he saw in his mirror, whose sufferings he well knew. Perhaps that is the reason for the objective humility of these self-portraits.

B.N. — Your own humility is to take the head of another...

L. le B. — No, that's my curiosity, my burning curiosity in this other which has something to do with me, which is a superior version of myself...

Translated from the original French.
Introspect, Dublin 1977

[15]

2 IMAGE OF W.B. YEATS 1975

[16]

4 IMAGE OF W.B. YEATS 1975, (DETAIL)

5
IMAGE OF
W.B. YEATS
1975, (DETAIL)

6
IMAGE OF
W.B. YEATS
1975, (DETAIL)

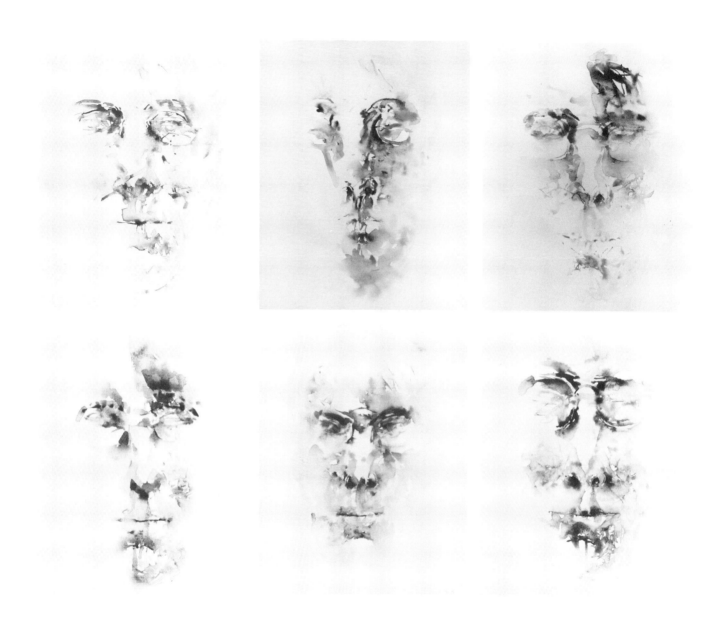

9 SIX STUDIES TOWARD AN IMAGE OF W.B. YEATS 1965

15 IMAGE OF JAMES JOYCE 1978, (DETAIL)

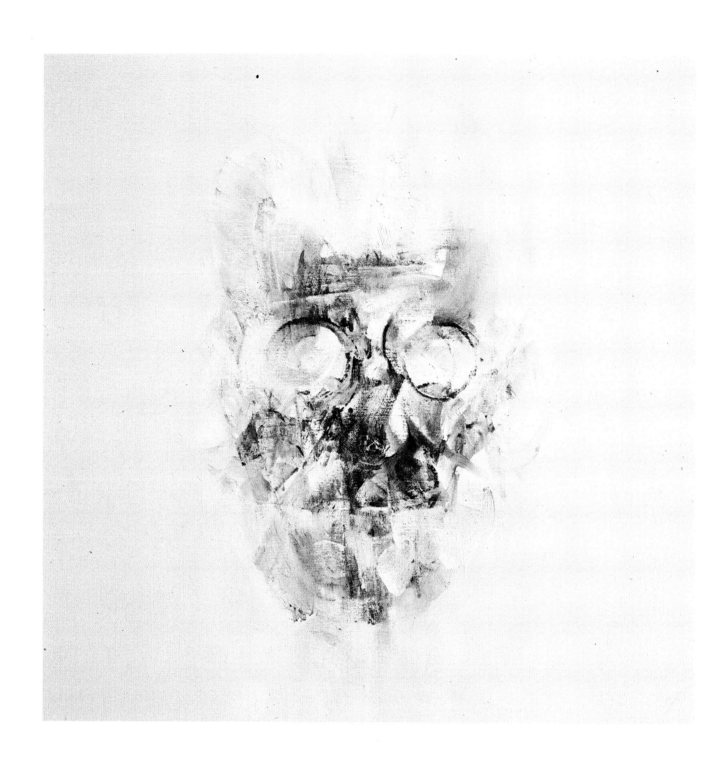

12 IMAGE OF JAMES JOYCE 1977, (DETAIL)

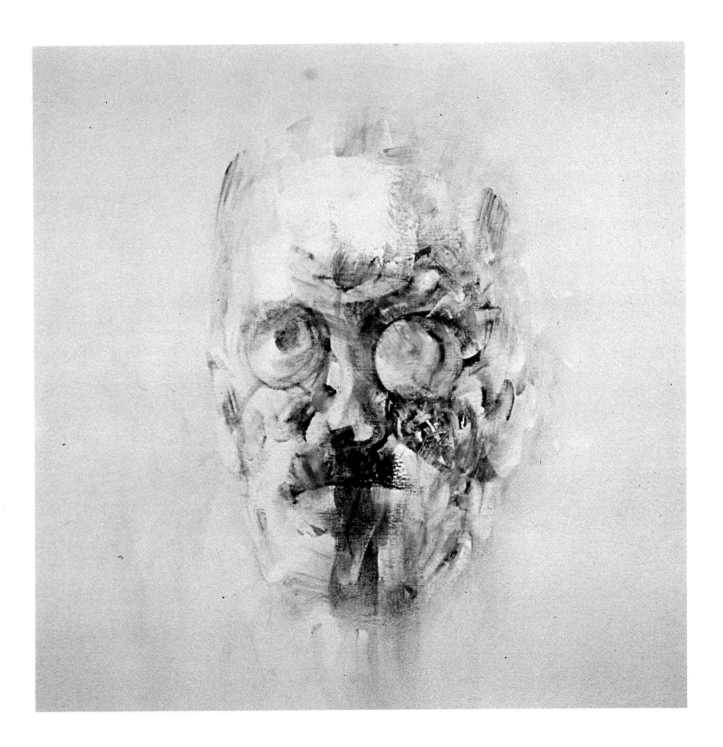

11 IMAGE OF JAMES JOYCE 1978, (DETAIL)

14 IMAGE OF JAMES JOYCE 1978, (DETAIL)

JAWEYES

Le Brocquy's fascination with Joyce does not follow from his many studies of Yeats; it precedes them. For how could a Dublin painter who lives abroad avoid contemplating our greatest exile? Having floated onto his canvas some thirteen years ago, the head of Dublin's mighty artificer now reappears in a luminous succession of aspects. This time it is not an Anglo-Irish but an aboriginal Irish face, obstinate and humorous, such as one might see along any bar counter, especially under that tilted hat. But he is also the first great artist of his race in the English language, the master forger of its conscience, born on St. Brigid's day, patroness of the hearth, the fire, the forge.

We see him short sighted, head bent to his work, draining the pus of the unconscious with his scalpel, "the cold steel pen". He robes in white, a doctor priest, to perform his detailed dissections of our secret lives. "I cannot write without offending people" he declares and shows us our daily selves and nightly fears, farts and all. The eyes are weak behind the enormous glasses but the jaw is a cliff of will. So the prognathous Irishman of Victorian caricature comes to conquer the language of the conqueror. "What is wrong with the English is that they always keep beating about the bush", he exclaims and raises his phallic monument in their own tongue.

His texts grow and grow, like an interlaced Celtic manuscript, corrections and additions serpenting along the margins. He scrutinises his spider's web, eyes agoggle like a racing driver, a sport which he is the only major writer to describe. Or an eyepatched pirate, Ireland's answer to Cromwell, marching the Victorian Muse into a brothel. Or a scientist, peering through his microscope at figures as large as life, his method "minutely analytic" as his suffering brother explains.

For we must never forget that he has endured that most heady of agonies, the surgeon's knife on the optic nerves. The brow is pain creased, the features lengthen or whiten, but even the pain cannot obliterate that fierce commitment. Sometimes the whole face seems smouldering, eyeballs scorched, portrait of the artist as a zealot, 'his long face red as an Indian's'.

So he drudges and dredges daily, and by nightfall he is free to be his other self, the level of white wine — electricity he calls it — rising and falling as darkness grows. They dine out, the only people he cares about, his family; and the friends who serve his work. Suddenly, he throws his head back, and his laughter rings around the restaurant. Before midnight his light tenor voice, once heard from the same platform as MacCormack, is raised in melody. If the work has been good, or the day attended by some success, he may dance, a thin dervish.

His whole being is a black mess, a bottlefield of contradictions. An Irishman who retains his British passport, he loathes British officialdom, and is obsessed with the land he left behind. He deserts the family into which he was born to create another to burden his reckless impoverished days. A faithful husband, he is fascinated by the idea of betrayal to the point of seeing Shakespeare as the cuckold King Hamlet. So the lean artificer, Daedalus, who echoes Satan's *non serviam*, grows into Bloom, humble, suffering, polite, a gentlemen of the old school, and finally Finnegan, the All Father.

For his antiseptic manner, affable but impenetrable, is the anti-mask of the artist. Sadness and gaiety, seriousness and anarchic humour, he makes his contradictions dance, a lecherous ascetic whose speech is both tender and coarse. Thin moustached, hair brushed back, he can look like a tight-lipped official or a tired professional out for a stroll, leaning on his cane. But a sudden twirl, and he is transformed into a variety artist, ready to trip and sing a seaside song. The mood shifts again, and it is a melancholy refrain, lost love or time past, his father's voice.

How much of our own poor selves we recognise in him, the ordinary made extraordinary! The youthful hater of the Rabblement ends as a great democrat of literature, fashioning a hymn for Everyman, thinking, excreting, loving, arguing, singing. These "left handed" manscapes, le Brocquy's re-invention of the portrait, link Joyce with the visual art of the race from which he sprang; link him to the strange beautiful heads, grim or grinning, of some early Celtic sanctuary or ruined Romanesque church. It is the stubborn face of Gaeldom, surviving all odds and vicissitudes, a light hearted joker with a heavy burden, wearing the invincible armour of self mockery.

JOHN MONTAGUE
Preface to catalogue, *Studies toward an image of James Joyce,* Gimpel Fils, exhibition touring Genoa, Zurich, London, Belfast, Dublin, New York, Montreal, Toronto, 1977-78. Art International, Vol. 22, Lugano 1978. The Crane Bag, Vol. 2 No. 1 & 2, Dublin 1978.

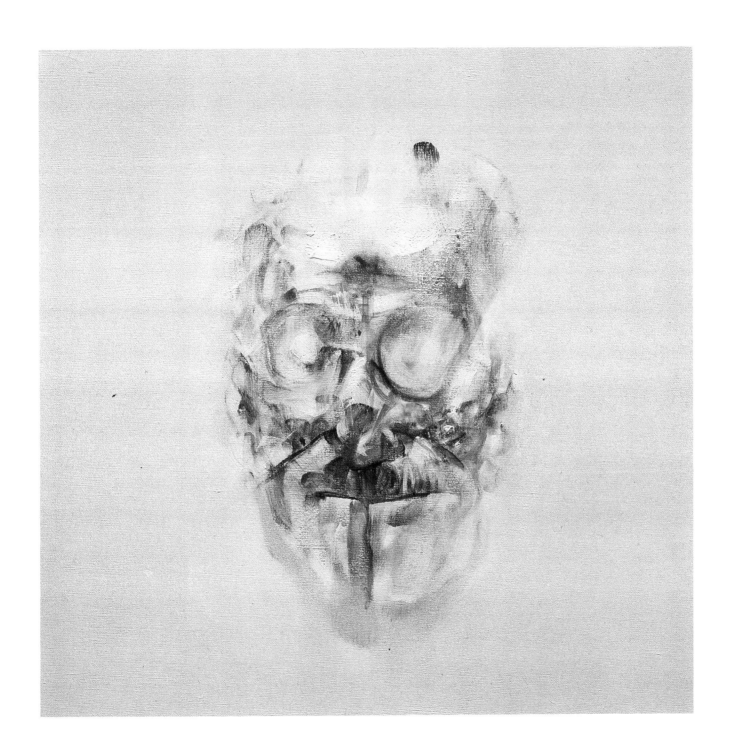

10 IMAGE OF JAMES JOYCE 1977, (DETAIL)

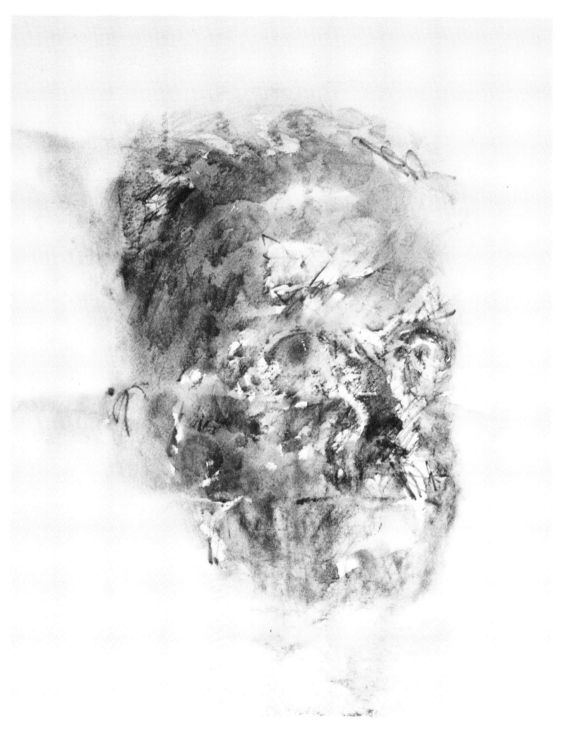

16
DETAIL OF
STUDIES TOWARD AN
IMAGE OF
JAMES JOYCE 1983,

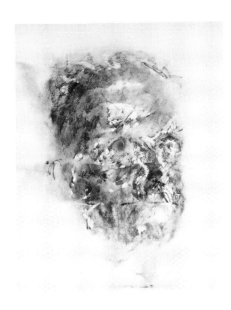

16 STUDIES TOWARD AN IMAGE OF JAMES JOYCE 1983

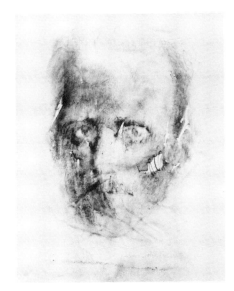

17 STUDIES TOWARD AN IMAGE OF JAMES JOYCE 1983

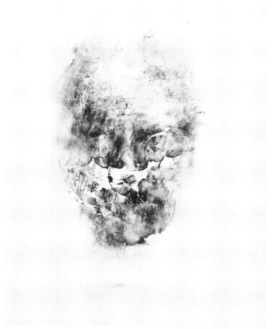

13
IMAGE OF
JAMES JOYCE
1978, (DETAIL)

Ever since I rediscovered for myself the image of the head, I have painted studies of James Joyce. I have never known Joyce, but am bound to him as a Dubliner. For it is said that no-one from that city can quite escape its microcosmic world, and I am certainly no exception. Joyce is the apotheosis, the archetype of our kind and it seems to me that in him — behind the volatile arrangement of his features — lies his unique evocation of that small city, large as life and therefore poignant everywhere. But to me, a Dublin man peering at Joyce, a particular nostalgia is added to the universal "epiphany" and this perhaps enables me to grope for something of my own particular experience within the ever-changing landscape of his face, within the various and contradictrory photographs of his head, within my bronze death-mask of him and, I suppose, within the recesses of my own mind.

L le B
Notes on Painting and Awareness,
Corps, Poésie, Peinture, Université de Nice, 8.02.1979.

For me, an Irishman, it was curiously enough the plays of Synge which provided the key to an understanding of Lorca's fierce lyrical world. Synge with his ear pressed against the floorboards, passionately noting the marvellous vernacular of the westerly people in the room below.

L le B
Notes on Painting and Awareness;
Corps, Poésie, Peinture, Université de Nice, 8.02.1979

24 IMAGE OF FEDERICO GARCIA LORCA 1978, (DETAIL)

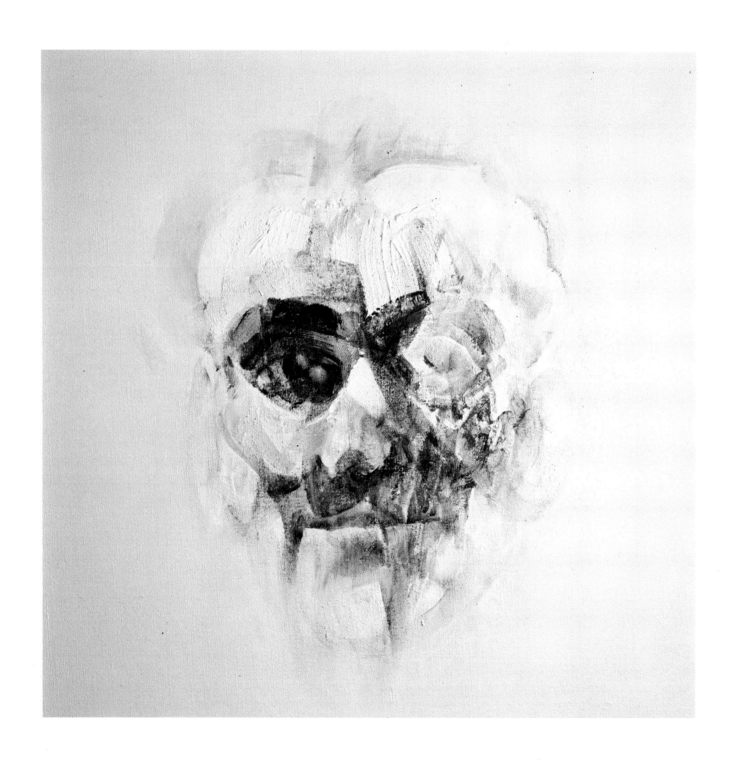

23 IMAGE OF FEDERICO GARCIA LORCA 1978, (DETAIL)

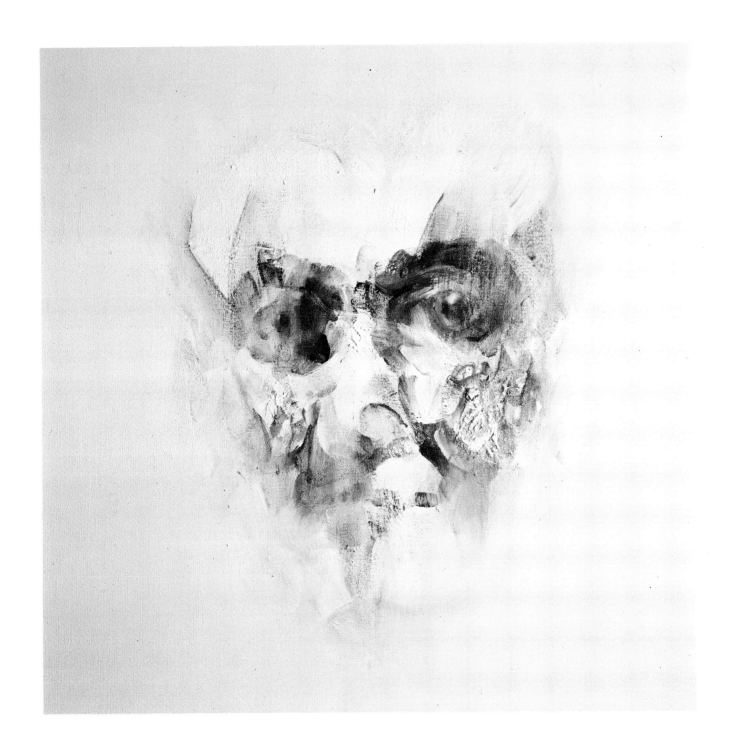

20 IMAGE OF FEDERICO GARCIA LORCA 1978, (DETAIL)

25 IMAGE OF FEDERICO GARCIA LORCA 1978, (DETAIL)

[36]

When Malevich painted his white-on-white pictures in 1917, he was seeking a means of signalling to the world that man's path lies through space, and he associated white with infinity. But the pioneering thrust of his Suprematist diagonals took another significance when it became a whiteness on white. The diagonals turned into ghostly presences and produced the optical effect of a partial emergence. The abstract suprematist emblem of human intrepidity was transformed into intimations of the numinous. Louis le Brocquy's white series is no less deeply involved in a concept of partial emergence, but that which partially emerges is identifiable as human — a human presence coming from yet still within and of the whiteness (like the Eurydice of Rilke's poem, full as a fruit with darkness) expanding circumspectly towards its indeterminable limits.

As I see it, when his textural treatment effaces the surface glitter of the white, and by effecting a kind of equation between opacity and transparency gives the painting an interior glow, he succeeds in transmogrifying his raw material, conveys to us something of his own sense of the mystery of the substance he is handling and even reminds us that the food miraculously provided for the Israelites on their pilgrimage through the wilderness was a white substance.

By adumbrating a human presence in his magic substance, le Brocquy seems to me to be challenging the now almost universally held belief that the concept of man in harmony with himself is spurious. Le Brocquy's paintings have helped me to realise that when Malevich said "I wish to be the maker of the new sign of my inner movement, for in me is the path of the world", it was much more than "avant-garde" effervescence, and that such a claim would be understood by, say, Erwin Schrödinger who has pointed out that consciousness is a singular of which the plural is unknown, and that what seems to be a plurality, is merely a series of different aspects of this one thing. Le Brocquy's vision of human presence in an infinite, undivided substance is an insight of the same order.

ROBERT MELVILLE

Extract from introduction to catalogue,
Louis le Brocquy,
Galerie Lienhard,
Zurich, 1961

[37]

"Accident is extremely important to me. I believe that my role as an artist, in so far as it exists, lies in the recognition of significant marks as they occur. And these are what I retain and expand, and from which I hope an image will emerge. To me painting is *not* a means of communication or even self-expression, but rather a process of discovering, or uncovering. I think of the painter as a kind of archaeolgist, an archaeologist of the spirit, patiently disturbing the surface of things until he makes a discovery which will enable him to take his search further...

Well, what occurs, I think, is this. Successive marks made by a brush dipped in this and that pigment, almost at random, build up a kind of scribbled structure of colour in and out of the features of the image which is gradually forming. Then this free structure usually suggests the areas where white pigment may be heavily brushed on to form the outer planes of the image. But each plane and each coloured mark, whether sharp in contour or melting, has to have its autonomy — its independence, if you like, of any merely descriptive role. And these marks have to coexist independently within the various depths of the landscape of the head-image. They have to be allowed, as it were, to float within it...

A great deal of the technical difficulty in these paintings comes from the fact that they are heads in utter isolation — without any particular circumstances, such as a collar and tie, or a recognizable background. Now the difficult thing in my view is to make this isolated head so that it doesn't look like a mere sketch, which it isn't, nor like some kind of decapitation. The image has to emerge from a plausible matrix, beyond habitual circumstance or environment, as if outside time. You may have noticed that there are no circumstantial details in the images — barely even any hair, which I consider circumstantial, since it can be long or short, or indicative of a young or old man, and these are comments which I wish to avoid.

Louis le Brocquy, replying to Michael Peppiatt, Art International, October 1979.

[38]

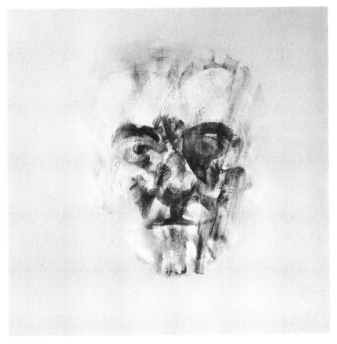

21 IMAGE OF FEDERICO GARCIA LORCA 1978, (DETAIL)

22 IMAGE OF FEDERICO GARCIA LORCA 1978, (DETAIL)

26 IMAGE OF FEDERICO GARCIA LORCA 1978, (DETAIL)

27 IMAGE OF FEDERICO GARCIA LORCA 1978, (DETAIL)

28
IMAGE OF
FEDERICO
GARCIA LORCA
1978-86, (DETAIL)

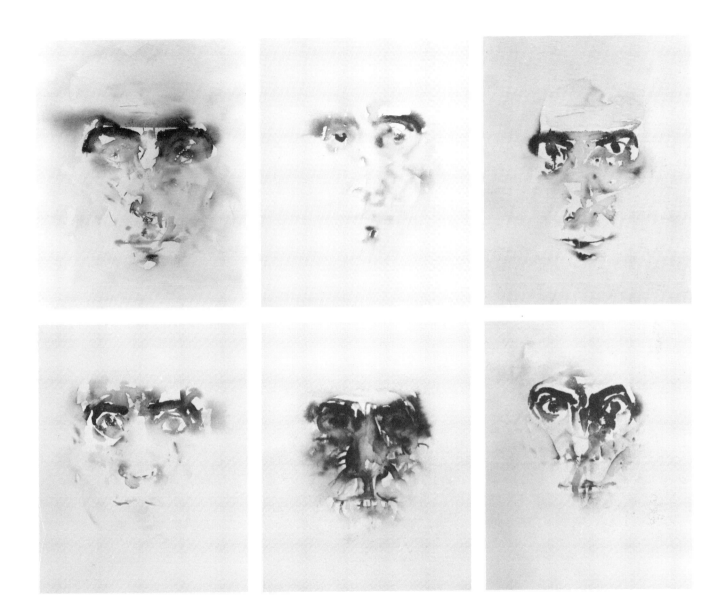

30 SIX STUDIES TOWARD AN IMAGE OF FEDERICO GARCIA LORCA 1977

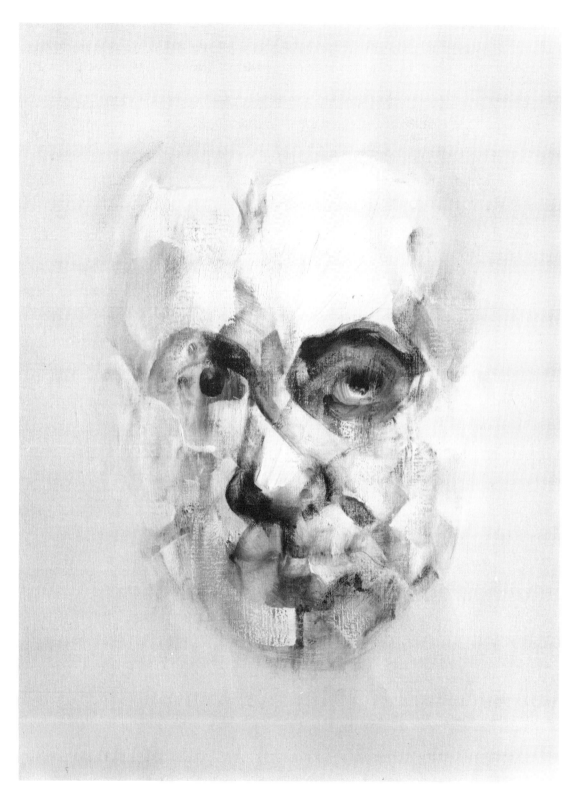

29
IMAGE OF
FEDERICO
GARCIA LORCA
1978, (DETAIL)

Osip Mandelstam, in his extraordinary *Conversation about Dante*, says: "A quotation is not an excerpt. A quotation is a cicada. Its natural state is that of unceasing sound. Having once seized hold of the air, it will not let it go."

Louis le Brocquy's heads are in this way quotations from bodies, from lives even. We have no sense of them orphaned from their supporting frames or times. They take hold of the air, they probe it with a deep pure stare.

They are complete; they have come through. They assist with a displacing confidence, as if they have returned early from fulfilling commands we did not expect them to fulfil, and are attending now within the calm of their own achievement.

However, if the images house that impassive satisfaction, the image-maker knows no such repose. He is pestered by new commands that disturb the repose once it has been found, and he is under *geasa* until he has found it again, like some Dantean shade doomed to hunger after form even as forms swim in and out of touch:

> For last year's words belong to last year's language And next year's
> words await another voice

The lyric poem has been called "a way of putting it" and "a momentary stay". There is an element of the accidental about it as well as a sense of inevitability. It is as much a result of the poet's language generating itself as of the poet expressing himself. So it is altogether proper that Louis le Brocquy's images of poets should stand in relation to their poems, because these images also take delight in caging the moment, staying the accident. The rhythm of composition, in both cases, is the one suggested by Robert Frost's neat and jubilant triad: "Sight. Excite. Insight". Le Brocquy has written sympathetically about James Joyce's "unique boat-shaped head — the raised poop of the forehead the jutting bow of the jaw — within which he made his heroic voyage, his *navigatio*". The metaphor calls up an answering one, of le Brocquy's own spirit "unappeased and peregrine" making its *navigatio* in the light currach of his hand dipping and swirling on the horizonless paper. "There is a brain in the hand," he says. "A handprint is a personality".

Yet that hand does not seek to express its own personality. It is obedient rather than dominant, subdued into process as it awaits a discovery. What it comes up with will sometimes feel like something come upon, a recognition. Like a turfcutter's spade coming upon the body in the bog, the head of the Tollund Man, ghostly yet palpable, familiar and other, a historical creature grown ahistorical, an image that has seized hold of the eye and will not let it go.

SEAMUS HEANEY
From *Eight Irish Writers*, eight poems in a portfolio of collotype lithographs, edited by Andrew Carpenter, Dublin 1981.

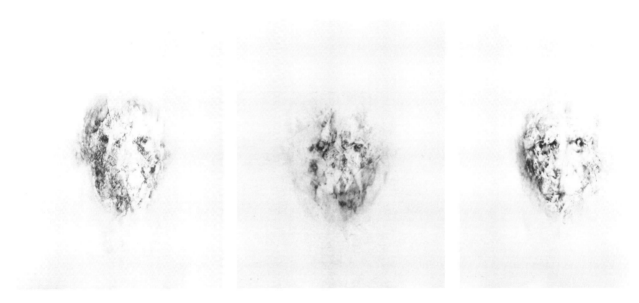

35 STUDIES TOWARD AN IMAGE OF PABLO PICASSO 1983

"Fame and photography have made Picasso's remarkable head familiar to us all. Each one of us has formed an image of his face. Yet the face itself remains ambiguous, both masking and revealing a consciousness too explosive to be wholly contained within its exterior appearance. And so I have not attempted to paint the appearance, the material fact of Picasso. On the contrary, I have deliberately effaced the well-known likeness so that from the depths of that palimpsest might emerge some ulterior image of this extraordinary man".

L le B
From the Film, *Another Way of Knowing*
by Michael Garvey, RTE 1986

31 IMAGE OF PICASSO 1983, (DETAIL)

33 IMAGE OF PICASSO 1983, (DETAIL)

34 IMAGE OF PICASSO 1983, (DETAIL)

32 IMAGE OF PICASSO

JANUS

Faces that cannot escape themselves. Insomniac. Dividing into multiple selves. Upsetting the composure of self-identity. Only given cohesion by the look of the other — by each one of us who stands before these faces. Vigilant.

But who is looking and who is looked at? Is not our own sense of selfhood put into question by these painted faces? Suspending our disbelief — our secure knowledge that these are only fictional tracings — do we not enter into a mirror play? Do we not discover our own vulnerability staring back at us from the canvas? The wounded eyes at once an accusation and a plea. Coming forward from their coloured mask in entreaty. Withdrawing again in ambiguity. Hesitancy. Emergence and immergence.

Paintings of ambivalence. Exposure of depth on surface. Janus disclosed, looking in two directions at once. Inwards towards the self; outwards towards the other. The self that knows that self is not enough. The self that knows that it is obsessed by the other. The self that admits: *je est un autre.*

The paintings speak for themselves. The artist has disappeared so that these faces can appear. The generosity of creation, of emptying oneself so that the creatures can come into being, with a life of their own. Kenosis. But once he has created, the artist has as much reason as another to speak about his work. Another kind of generosity this: post-natal, perhaps even posthumous. This is what le Brocquy has written of his paintings, of ambivalence: "Such a concept of a disseminated consciousness surpassing personality would, I imagine, produce an ambiguity involving a dislocation of our conception of time (within which coming and going, beginning and end, are normally regarded) and transforming this "normal" view by the addition of a contrary sense of simultaneity or timelessness. In my own small world of painting, I have learned that emergence and immergence are ambivalent: that one implies the other and that the state or matrix in which they co-exist apparently dissolves the sense of time, producing a characteristic *stillness.*[1]

This dismantling of historical time is a central feature of postmodern art.

The modernist belief in each art movement or art work as a leap into the new, its rejection of past paradigms in the name of something absolutely original, is being challenged. The idea of the *avant garde* as the artistic equivalent to the Onward March of History has had its day. The modern cult of inevitable *Progress* is being replaced by the post-modern notion of history as *collage*: different styles and images drawn from past and present.

Le Brocquy's head series are post-modern in this sense. They represent a curious blending of the old and the new, the ancient and the modern. At one level, they depict great minds of modern art — Yeats, Joyce, Lorca, Picasso, Beckett, Bacon. Yet at another, they look back (as le Brocquy informs us) to the ancient sculptured heads of Celto-Ligurian Entremont and of Romanesque Clonfert.[2] The end of Western art is thus superimposed on its beginning. Linear chronology is deconstructed into an ambivalent co-existence of different time-frames. But this superimposition of present on past is here seen inversely, taking the form of an archaeology which strips away the surface layers of skin to reveal the buried bone structures beneath. Le Brocquy's head excavations are portraits of the modern artist as an ancient man, explorations of cultural memory, reminders that visions of the future must be grounded in recollection.

This double vision, this temporal ambivalence, is not something invented by le Brocquy. It is discovered within the very artistic consciousnes of those he portrays. In Beckett's work he discovers that "going is confounded with coming, backwards with forwards". In Yeats he perceives a system of reincarnation where the present implies the past: a motif captured in the image of the winding stair at Thoor Ballylee, "climbed and descended repeatedly". And in Joyce he finds the convergence of dayconsciousness and nightconsciousness, of the modern-day Finnegan and the mythological Fionn Macool — "the continual presence of the historic past, the indivisibility of birth and funeral, spanning the apparent chasm between past and present".[3]

Le Brocquy's invocation of an historic past which haunts the consciousness of many of his compatriot artists, has nothing to do with *revivalism*. On the contrary, any claim of triumphalistic nationalism is radically subverted. These faces are not self- possessed. They are not sure of themselves. They are searchingly insecure, shifting, restive. Yeats, Joyce, Beckett return to us as aliens, exiles, refugees, nomads. They represent that unsettling blend of the familiar and the foreign which Joyce declared to be the mark of the Irish writer in English. Their faces, like their works and their culture, are unashamedly *plural*. They resist the reductive frame of a single image. Disseminating faces that cannot be pinned down, that explode representation, initiating a series of images that is, in principal, endless. If the origin of cultural identity is being explored, it is as a fall-out of traces — a diaspora that cannot be retraced to a homeland. The very notion of identity deconstructs itself before our eyes. These faces are questions, not answers.

Le Brocquy's post-modern balancing of the old and the new is also manifest in the *iconic* nature of his paintings. While these faces ostensibly recall the sacramental status of ancient Byzantine icons, there is another contemporary allusion at work: the allusion to the mass-produced icons of photography. Le Brocquy himself stated that his multiple studies towards an image remain an unending task. And for this reason: "to attempt today a portrait, a single static image of a great artist like Joyce seems to me futile as well as impertinent. Long conditioned by photography and the cinema... we now perceive the human individual as facetted, kinetic". Le Brocquy suggests, furthermore, that this multiplication of the image into an indefinite series without beginning or end is essentially *counter-Renaissance*. It introduces a multiple vision that is "cyclic rather than linear, repetitive yet simultaneous and, above all, inconclusive".[4]

Le Brocquy's head series may thus be viewed in accordance with the general post-modern tendency to deconstruct the Renaissance legacy of representation and composition, a legacy which deeply informs the aesthetic conventions of modernity. Le Brocquy's multi-series replaces the notion of *resemblance* with that of *similitude*. Resemblance, as the traditional model of representation, presupposes a "primary reference" of image to reality: here the image is a "copy" which faithfully imitates its original. Similitude, by contrast, subverts the idea of representational reference, with its hierarchy of origin and imitation: here the image is set loose from any privileged model, reproducing itself in a series of lateral repetitions. Similitude "circulates the simulacrum as the indefinite and reversible relation of the similar to the similar".[5] Applying this post-modern category of similitude to the Andy Warhol serigraphs of media faces and images, Michel Foucault observes how we witness a dissolution of the idea of a unique model or original: "by means of similitude relayed indefinitely along the length of a series, the image itself, along with the name it bears, loses its identity. Campbell, Campbell, Campbell, Campbell".[6]

Clearly there is no direct analogy between Warhol's serigraphs of commodity images like Campbell Soup cans or Marilyn Monroe faces and le Brocquy's multiple series of artists' heads. Le Brocquy is concerned with an archaeological exploration of the *hidden spirit* of these artists whereas Warhol is playing with the idea that technologically reproducible media images can be pressured into significance by simultaneous repetition and *surface imitation*. But comparison is not entirely impertinent at the level of form. Both le Brocquy and Warhol are responding instinctively to the postmodern discovery (made in structuralist and post-structuralist theories of language) that signs do not refer to objects in any fixed or determinate manner. Using familiar images — such as Marilyn Monroe or Joyce — in such a way that the viewer is compelled to question the rapport between such images and their originals, artists as widely different as le Brocquy and Warhol are undermining our inherited assumptions about representation. By reproducing an almost random series of images, these artists decompose the Renaissance and indeed Romantic cult of an authentic original. Or to put it another way, the relationship between image and reality, copy and model, is rendered undecidable. Disinherited of our certainties and dispossessed of our convenient assumptions about perception, we the viewers of such serial images no longer look in the same way. We are exposed to *otherness*. We see *otherwise*.

Neither religious icons nor photographic reproductions, le Brocquy's multi-facetted faces keep vigil. They cannot be fixed, defined, explained. Condemned to silence. Look at those eyes. Sleepless. Their looking cannot end. They cannot close. And they will not let us alone, close ourselves off, shut down for the night. They appeal to us to keep our eyes open too, to keep on looking, to keep watch. Each of le Brocquy's multiple faces echoes the vow of Beckett's unnameable narrator: "I can't go on, I'll go on".

RICHARD KEARNEY
DUBLIN, 1987

NOTES

1) Louis le Brocquy. *A Painter's Notes on Ambivalence* in The Crane Bag Book of Irish Studies, Blackwater Press, Dublin, 1982 p.151-2.
2) *Ibid* p152
3) *Ibid* p152
4) Louis le Brocquy. *Notes on Painting and Awareness* in "Painting and Poetry", Symposium, Nice University, 1979
5) Michel Foucault, *This is Not a Pipe*, University of California Press, 1983 p10.
6) *Ibid* p53-54

[52]

36
IMAGE OF
SAMUEL BECKETT
1979, (DETAIL)

37
IMAGE OF
SAMUEL BECKETT
1979, (DETAIL)

38
IMAGE OF
SAMUEL BECKETT
1980, (DETAIL)

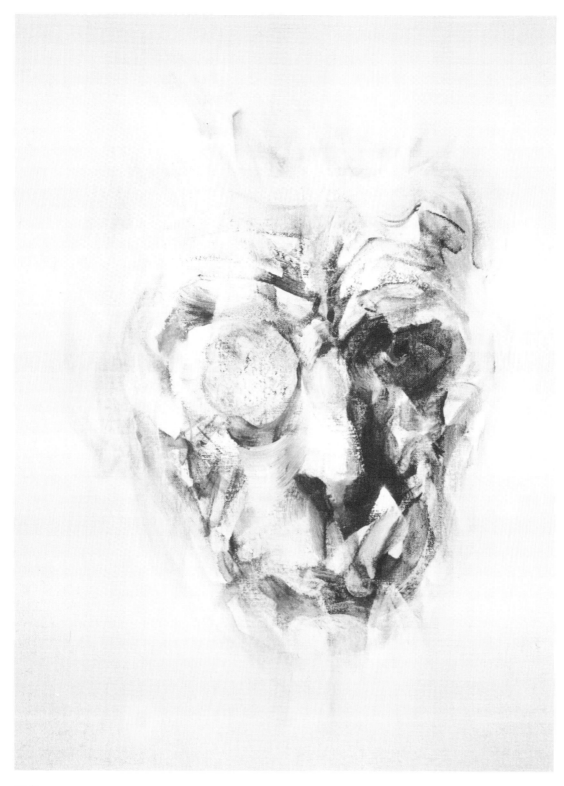

39
IMAGE OF
SAMUEL BECKETT
1982, (DETAIL)

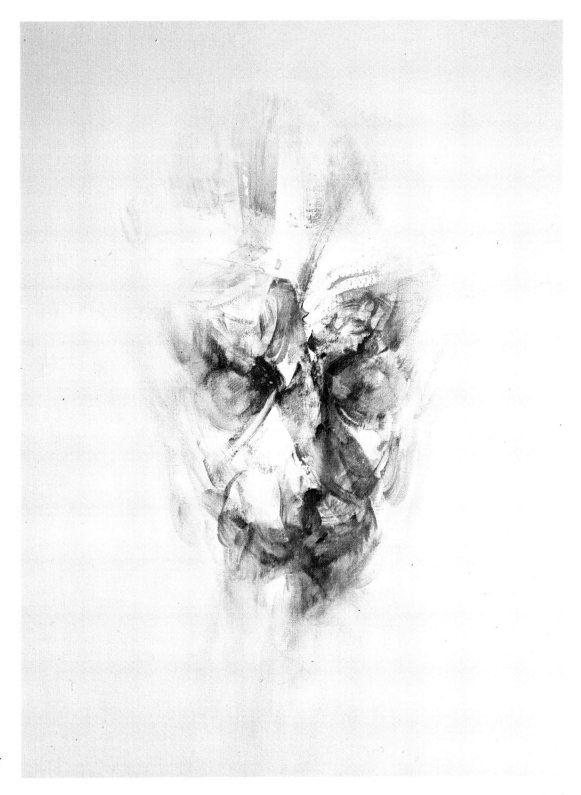

41
IMAGE OF
SAMUEL BECKETT
1987, (DETAIL)

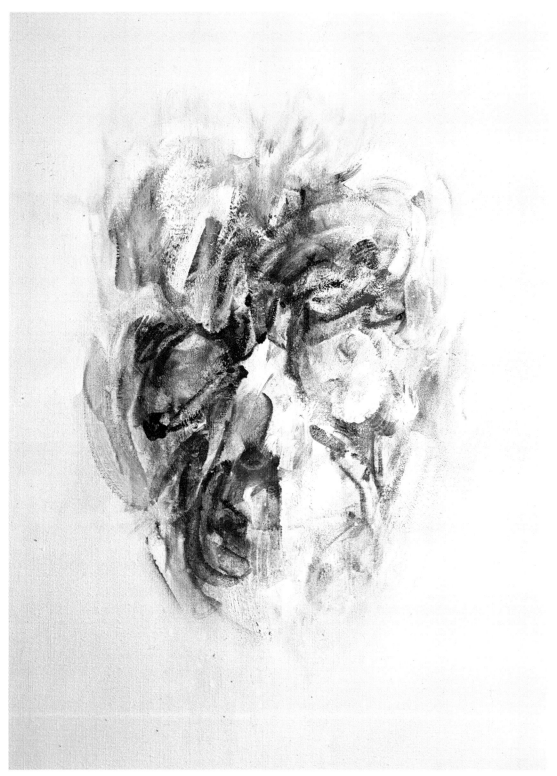

43
IMAGE OF
SAMUEL BECKETT
1987, (DETAIL)

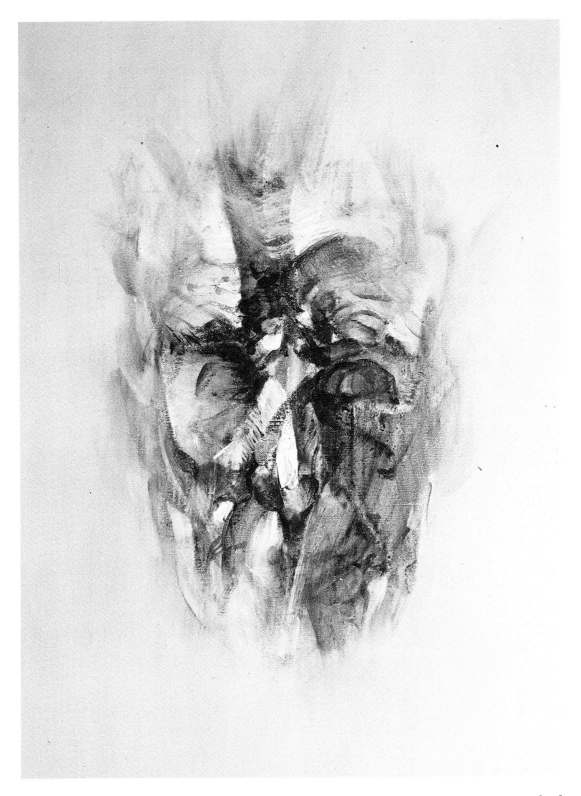

42
IMAGE OF
SAMUEL BECKETT
1987, (DETAIL)

40 IMAGE OF SAMUEL BECKETT 1982, (DETAIL)

44 SIX STUDIES TOWARD AN IMAGE OF SAMUEL BECKETT 1980

"When painting either the torso or the head there was always this concentration on the individual coupled with a conviction, which may seem banal, that the final human reality is the individual. It appears obvious, but today people seem to align themselves in groups and factions, and seem to suffer in groups and factions so that we may almost forget that the individual repeats itself from one group or faction to another and into another...

I like to start out a number of things at once, push them out, and I often find that I make whatever small breakthroughs I do rather spontaneously and immediately on returning to a painting where I've developed a problem. I would say, on the whole, I'm not prolific. I discard a lot and destroy a great deal, I'm a rather jumpy, erratic painter in fact. I make discoveries, such as they are, while painting; the painting dictates to an enormous extent, it may seem to be considered, deliberate, but in point of fact it is almost autonomous, emerging gradually under one's hands and not because of them...

The quality which I think I admire most in a painter, and try to induce in myself, is *stamina*. Wasn't it the struggle of Jacob and the Angel? The absolutely necessary commitment of the painter to his material, in which he can be almost destroyed by his material, in which he can die into his material. His own personality is thus not imposed but is really overcome, transformed. There is something in the struggle with the material in which the personality is — it sounds rather mystic — reborn in the form of this new convention, this painterly restatement of the reality which preoccupies the artist. It's a very difficult struggle and it's not one which always comes off. Sometimes the painter breaks away from the struggle and comes away with nothing, he has neither succumbed nor been victorious in any sense. These are the moments when the work, which is in fact a record of the struggle, is destroyed by the artist, rejected".

Extract from *Harriet Cooke talks to Louis le Brocquy*, Irish Times 25.5.1973

Le Brocquy came to heads, as a general subject, by way of two quite separate cultures, neither of them part of the traditional mainstream of European art. There was a head-cult of Celto -Ligurian origin that had been practised near Aix-en-Provence, and there was a group of Melanesian- Polynesian images, now in the Musée de l'Homme in Paris. These latter images were made, according to le Brocquy's own description, of "skulls, partly remodelled with clay, and then painted in a decorative way, often with cowrie shells for eyes". This notion of the human head as something that could be remodelled and painted over was the source of at least one substantial painting in 1964, and the notion of the ancestral head as something to be summoned up — complete or incomplete, remodelled or frankly in ruins — was the subject of a whole group of paintings in 1964-65. Common to all this activity was the idea of the head as something supremely important that could legitimately be built and re-built, patched and re-patched. The heads thus constructed could also have an ancestral quality and serve, therefore, as models, exemplars, and dictionaries of virtue. And the heads in those transitional paintings do indeed have the battered, fragmented, voiceless and sightless look that we recognize in so many of the human images that have come down to us in much-mutilated marble.

But those qualities were quite irrelevant to the task that le Brocquy set himself from 1975 onwards. Even the evocation of the massed heads in the Romanesque abbey of Clonfert, in Galway, did not quite prepare him for the ordeal of bringing W.B. Yeats back to life. It so happens that Louis le Brocquy as a boy had personal contacts with Yeats as someone who knew his mother in Dublin and could be met in this house or that. He had, therefore, a first-hand contact that could be said to make his task easier. But to have "met" a great writer does not always make it easier to understand his work. Nor did Yeats look the same throughout his life...

So Yeats was a good test. Louis le Brocquy stalked him with a long patience, trapping first one and then another aspect of one of the least easily definable of men. "Painting is groping and watching", he said not long ago, and the words exactly describe the process of his paintings of heads. "When you are painting", he said, "you want to discover, to uncover, to reveal".

JOHN RUSSELL
Extract from his introduction to *Louis le Brocquy*, Dorothy Walker,
Ward River, Dubin 1981. Hodder & Stoughton, London 1982.

50
STUDIES TOWARD
AN IMAGE OF
FRANCIS BACON
1982

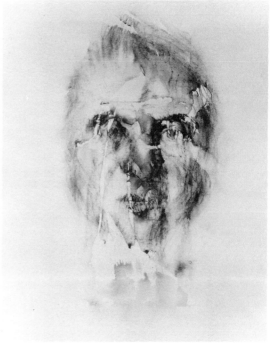

51
STUDIES TOWARD
AN IMAGE OF
FRANCIS BACON
1982

46
IMAGE OF
FRANCIS BACON
1979, (DETAIL)

52
STUDY TOWARDS
AN IMAGE OF
FRANCIS BACON
1980

47
IMAGE OF
FRANCIS BACON
1979-86, (DETAIL)

45
IMAGE OF
FRANCIS BACON
1979-86, (DETAIL)

45
IMAGE OF
FRANCIS BACON
1979, (DETAIL)

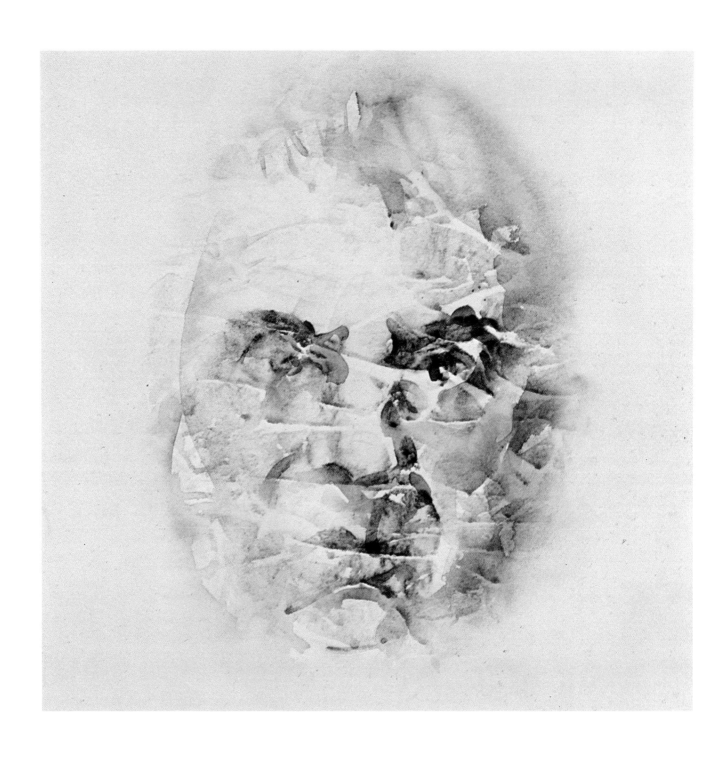

52 STUDY TOWARDS AN IMAGE OF FRANCIS BACON 1980

48 IMAGE OF FRANCIS BACON 1985, (DETAIL)

49
IMAGE OF
FRANCIS BACON
1985, (DETAIL)

BIOGRAPHIC NOTE

Louis le Brocquy was born in Dublin of Irish parents on 10th November 1916. In 1938, when he was almost twenty two, he abruptly left Ireland and his grandfather's business to become a painter. With no formal training he studied on his own at the London National Gallery, the Louvre, in Venice and at Geneva — then the temporary home of the Prado. "He was enthralled by Spanish painting and its influence has remained a feature of his work, where the precision of his tone values and his use of grey and white, both very prominent factors in Spanish painting, are constantly important".[1]

He returned through France to Ireland in 1940, where, in 1945, his early work was remarked by Charles Gimpel. In 1947 le Brocquy exhibited with the new Gimpel Fils Gallery in London, where he worked for a decade and became well known as a younger member of a very diverse contemporary group, including Nicholson, Adler, Sutherland, Pasmore, Scott and Bacon.

During this time, le Brocquy's developing art underwent a series of radical changes. His paintings of the late forties of archetypal Irish tinker women — somewhat recalling de Kooning's later images — gave way to a stark, grey period, peopled by figures which, though usually grouped, produced the impression of isolation. This period was represented in *50 Ans d'Art Moderne*, Brussels World Fair, 1958, by his large painting *A Family*, which had previously been awarded a major international prize at the 1956 Venice Biennale.

In 1958, he married the young Irish painter, Anne Madden, and left London to work with her in the comparative isolation of the French Midi. In that year, he began his long series of white paintings, referring to which the late Sir Herbert Read wrote: "This painter from Joyce's Dublin did seem when I first met him in 1944 to have some qualities of Celtic origin. His images might have been found in a crock of gold and both Yeats the poet and his brother the painter might have been among his ancestors. But since then le Brocquy's art has become emancipated from provincial myth and is now both independent and universal. He is a painter of the

LOUIS LE BROCQUY 1987.

inner world of feeling and has become most curiously original. His work (as perhaps all original work) reconciles two opposed principles, which I will tentatively call innocence and experience.

There can be no doubt that after many patient years of research this painter has found the irreducible symbols for what is basic to the life of the spirit, those principles we personify as Eros and Thanatos. Further investigation of this symbolism would be clumsy. It is preferable to remain on the sensuous surface, so lyrical, so lucid and so deft''.[2] These latter paintings yielded from their white matrix first torsos and corporeal imagery, implying a human presence, and then — from 1964 — a succession of anonymous "ancestral heads", giving way in 1975 to the current series of head images reflecting various painters and writers, including Samuel Beckett with whom the le Brocquys had formed a lasting friendship.

Important illustrated works by le Brocquy include Kinsella's renowned translation of *The Táin* in 1969, Andrew Carpenter's *Eight Irish Writers,* 1981 with drawings of Yeats, Synge, Joyce and the artist's friends, Francis Stuart, Samuel Beckett, Thomas Kinsella, John Montague and Seamus Heaney and, in 1986, Joyce's *Dubliners*.

It is difficult to categorise le Brocquy's work. From the first, he has been a lone painter, tending to stand apart from schools and movements. It may be said that he is related to that tradition within European painting in which an ambivalent role is played by the paint itself, at once insistent on its own nature while evocative of further imagery. His friend Francis Bacon's view (1966) is that 'Louis le Brocquy belongs to a category of artists who have always existed — obsessed by figuration outside and on the other side of illustration — who are aware of the vast and potent possibilities of inventing ways by which fact and appearance can be reconjugated''.

Le Brocquy is a hard critic of his own work, much of which he has rejected in the past. In the year 1963, he is known to have destroyed virtually his entire production of over forty oil paintings. Paradoxically perhaps for a painter of his temperament, he has engaged in a good deal of industrial design and was elected a Fellow of the UK Society of Industrial Artists and Designers in 1960. In 1962 he was awarded an honorary degree of Doctor of Literature by the University of Dublin. He was made Chevalier de la Légion d'Honneur in 1975.

In 1976 the Musée d'Art Moderne de la Ville de Paris exhibited a hundred studies towards an image of W. B. Yeats by le Brocquy. The New York State Museum held an extensive exhibition in 1981 of a hundred and twenty relevant works entitled *Louis le Brocquy and the Celtic Head Image*. In 1982 the Palais des Beaux-Arts, Charleroi, exhibited an important retrospective of his paintings and tapestries.

This present exhibition, assembled by the Arts Councils in Ireland, will be exhibited in 1987 at the Guinness Hop Store, Dublin and the Ulster Museum, Belfast, and, under the aegis of the National Gallery of Victoria, at the Westpac Gallery, of the Victoria Arts Centre, Melbourne 1988. The sixty minute film, *Louis le Brocquy. An Other Way of Knowing*, was made by RTE in 1986, directed by Michael Garvey in both English and French versions. It was first screened in Ireland on the artist's 70th birthday.

[1] Anne Crookshank, Professor of Art History, Trinity College, Dublin; *Le Brocquy Retrospective*, Municipal Gallery of Modern Art, Dublin 1966; Ulster Museum of Art, Belfast 1967.

[2] A Letter to a Young Painter, Herbert Read, Thames and Hudson, London 1962.

LIST OF WORKS

1. IMAGE OF W.B. YEATS 1975

Oil on canvas (385) 70 x 70 cm

exhibited
Arts Council of Northern Ireland
  Belfast, 1976
Crawford Municipal Gallery, Cork
  1976
Musée d'Art Moderne de la Ville de
  Paris 1976
Edinburgh International Festival
  (Demarco Gallery) 1977
New York State Museum 1981
Boston College, Mass. 1982
Westfield College, Mass. 1982
Palais des Beaux Arts, Charleroi 1982

private collection
illustrated on page 10

2. IMAGE OF W.B. YEATS 1975

Oil on Canvas (389) 70 × 70 cms

exhibited
Arts Council of Northern Ireland,
  Belfast 1976
Crawford Municipal Gallery, Cork
  1976
Musée d'Art Moderne de la Ville de
  Paris 1976
Edinburgh International Festival
  (Demarco Gallery) 1977
New York State Museum 1981
Boston College, Mass. 1982
Westfield College, Mass. 1982
Palais des Beaux Arts, Charleroi 1982

private collection
illustrated on page 16

3. IMAGE OF W.B. YEATS 1975

Oil on Canvas, (387) 70 x 70 cms

exhibited
Arts Council of Northern Ireland,
  Belfast 1976
Crawford Municipal Gallery, Cork
  1976
d'Art Moderne de la Ville de
  Paris 1976
Edinburgh International Festival
  (Demarco Gallery) 1977
New York State Museum 1981
Boston College, Mass. 1982
Westfield College, Mass. 1982
Palais des Beaux Arts, Charleroi 1982

collection
Mrs. Mary Heffernan
illustrated on page 11

4. IMAGE OF W.B. YEATS 1975

Oil on canvas (388) 70 x 70 cms

exhibited
Arts Council of Northern Ireland,
  Belfast 1976
Crawford Municipal Gallery, Cork
  1976
Musée d'Art Moderne de la Ville de
  Paris 1976
Edinburgh International Festival
  (Demarco) 1977
New York State Museum 1981
Boston College, Mass. 1982
Westfield College, Mass. 1982
Palais des Beaux Arts, Charleroi 1982

collection
Dr A.J.F. O'Reilly
illustrated on page 17

5. IMAGE OF W.B. YEATS 1975

Oil on canvas (389) 70 x 70 cms

exhibited
Arts Council of Northern Ireland,
  Belfast 1976
Crawford Municipal Gallery, Cork
  1976
Musée d'Art Moderne de la Ville de
  Paris 1976
Edinburgh International Festival
  (Demarco) 1977
New York State Museum 1981
Boston College, Mass. 1982
Westfield College, Mass. 1982
Palais des Beaux Arts, Charleroi 1982

private collection
illustrated on page 18

6. IMAGE OF W.B. YEATS 1975

Oil on canvas, (391) 70 x 70 cm

exhibited
Arts Council of Northern Ireland,
  Belfast 1976
Crawford Municipal Gallery, Cork
  1976
Musée d'Art Moderne de la Ville de
  Paris 1976
Edinburgh International Festival
  (Demarco) 1977
New York State Museum 1981
Boston College, Mass. 1982
Westfield College, Mass. 1982
Palais des Beaux Arts, Charleroi 1982

private collection
illustrated on page 19

7. IMAGE OF W.B. YEATS 1975

Oil on canvas, (392) 70 x 70 cms

exhibited
Arts Council of Northern Ireland,
  Belfast 1976
Crawford Municipal Gallery, Cork
  1976
Musée d'Art Moderne de la Ville de
  Paris 1976
Edinburgh International Festival
  (Demarco) 1977
New York State Museum 1981
Boston College, Mass. 1982
Westfield College, Mass. 1982
Palais des Beaux Arts, Charleroi 1982

private collection
illustrated on page 9

8. IMAGE OF W.B. YEATS 1981

Oil on canvas, (466) 80 x 80 cms

exhibited
Artists for Amnesty, auction, Bank of
  Ireland Dublin 1982

private collection
illustrated on page 12

9. SIX STUDIES TOWARD AN
IMAGE OF
W. B. YEATS, 1965

watercolour on paper
(w198) 22 x 18 cm
(w204) 22 x 18 cm
(w205) 22 x 18 cm
(w206) 22 x 18 cm
(w235) 22 x 18 cm
(w237) 22 x 18 cm

exhibited
Arts Council of Northern Ireland,
    Belfast 1976
Crawford Municipal Gallery, Cork
    1976
Musée D'Art Moderne de la Ville de
    Paris 1976
Edinburgh International Festival
    (Demarco) 1977
New York State Museum 1981
Palais des Beaux Arts, Charleroi 1982

private collection
illustrated on page 20

10. IMAGE OF JAMES JOYCE 1977

Oil on canvas (395) 70 x 70 cm

exhibited
Municipal Gallery of Modern Art,
Dublin 1978
Arts Council of Northern Ireland,
    Belfast 1978
New York State Museum 1981
Boston College 1982 Mass.
Westfield College, Mass. 1982
Palais des Beaux Arts, Charleroi 1982

private collection
illustrated on page 27

11. IMAGE OF JAMES JOYCE 1978

Oil on canvas (397) 70x70 cm

exhibited
Municipal Gallery of Modern Art,
Dublin 1978
Arts Council of Northern Ireland,
    Belfast 1978
New York State Museum 1981
Boston College, Mass. 1982

Westfield College, Mass. 1982
Palais des Beaux Arts, Charleroi 1982

private collection
illustrated on page 23

12. IMAGE OF JAMES JOYCE 1977

Oil on canvas (404) 146 x 114 cms

exhibited
Municipal Gallery of Modern Art,
    Dublin 1978
Arts Council of Northern Ireland,
    Belfast 1978
New York State Museum 1981
Boston College , Mass. 1982
Westfield College, Mass. 1982
Palais des Beaux Arts Charleroi 1982

collection
Ulster Museum, Belfast
illustrated on page 22

13. IMAGE OF JAMES JOYCE 1978

Oil on canvas (406) 70x70 cm

exhibited
Municipal Gallery of Modern Art,
Dublin 1978
Arts Council of Northern Ireland,
    Belfast 1978
New York State Museum 1981
Boston College, Mass. 1982
Westfield College, Mass. 1982
Palais des Beaux Arts Charleroi 1982

private collection
illustrated on page 31

14. IMAGE OF JAMES JOYCE 1978

Oil on canvas (426) 70x70 cm

exhibited
Municipal Gallery of Modern Art
Dublin 1978
Arts Council of Northern Ireland,
    Belfast 1978
New York State Museum 1981
Boston College, Mass. 1982
Westfield College, Mass. 1982
Palais des Beaux Arts, Charleroi 1982

private collection
illustrated on page 24

15. IMAGE OF JAMES JOYCE 1978

Oil on canvas (472) 80x80 cm

private collection
illustrated on page 21

16. STUDIES TOWARD AN IMAGE
OF JAMES JOYCE 1983 Triptych
(w665)

Watercolour and crayon on paper,
each 61 x 46 cms

private collection 29
illustrated on page 29
detail on page 28

17. STUDIES TOWARD AN IMAGE
OF JAMES JOYCE 1983 Triptych
(w679)

Watercolour and crayon on paper,
each 61 x 46 cms

private collection
illustrated on page 29

18. STUDIES TOWARD AN IMAGE
OF JAMES JOYCE 1983 Diptych
(w685)

Watercolour and crayon on paper
each 61 x 46 cms

private collection
illustrated on page 30

19. STUDIES TOWARDS AN IMAGE
OF JAMES JOYCE 1983 Diptych
(w690)

Watercolour and crayon on paper
each 61 x 46 cms

private collection
illustrated on page 30

20. IMAGE OF FEDERICO GARCIA
    LORCA 1978-83

Oil on canvas (408) 70 x 70 cm

originally exhibited
Galeria Maeght Barcelona 1978:
Kreisler-Dos, Madrid 1979
Fundacion Rodriguez-Acosta, Granada
 1979

private collection
illustrated on page 35

21. IMAGE OF FEDERICO GARCIA
LORCA 1978

Oil on canvas (409) 70 x 70 cms

exhibited
Galeria Maeght, Barcelona 1978:
Kreisler-Dos, Madrid 1979
Fundacion Rodriguez-Acosta, Granada
 1979
New York State Museum, 1981
Boston College, Mass. 1982
Westfield College, Mass. 1982
Palais des Beaux Arts, Charleroi 1982

private collection
illustrated on page 39

22. IMAGE OF FEDERICO GARCIA
LORCA 1978

Oil on canvas (410) 80 x 80 cm

exhibited
Galeria Maeght, Barcelona 1978:
Kreisler-Dos, Madrid 1979
Fundacion Rodriguez-Acosta, Granada
 1979
Musée des Arts Decoratifs, Paris 1979
New York State Museum 1981
Boston College, Mass. 1982
Westfield College, Mass. 1982
Palais des Beaux Arts, Charleroi 1982

private collection
illustrated on page 39

23. IMAGE OF FEDERICO GARCIA
LORCA 1978

Oil on canvas (411) 80 x 80 cms

exhibited
Galeria Maeght, Barcelona 1978:
Kreisler-Dos, Madrid 1979

Fundacion Rodriguez-Acosta, Granada
 1979
New York State Museum, 1981
Boston College, Mass. 1982
Westfield College, Mass. 1982
Palais des Beaux Arts, Charleroi 1982

private collection
illustrated on page 34

24. IMAGE OF FEDERICO GARCIA
LORCA 1978

Oil on canvas (412) 80 x 80 cm

exhibited
Galeria Maeght, Barcelona 1978:
Kreisler-Dos, Madrid 1979
Fundacion Rodriguez-Acosta, Granada
 1979
Musée des Arts Decoratifs, Paris 1979
New York State Museum, 1981
Boston College, Mass. 1982
Westfield College, Mass. 1982
Palais des Beaux Arts, Charleroi 1982
New York State Museum 1982

private collection
illustrated on page 33

25. IMAGE OF FEDERICO GARCIA
LORCA 1978

Oil on canvas (413) 80 x 80 cm

exhibited
Galeria Maeght, Barcelona 1978:
Kreisler-Dos, Madrid 1979
Fundacion Rodriguez-Acosta, Granada
 1979
New York State Museum 1981
Boston College, Mass. 1982
Westfield College, Mass. 1982
Palais des Beaux Arts, Charleroi 1982

private collection
illustrated on page 36

26. IMAGE OF FEDERICO GARCIA
LORCA 1978-86

Oil on canvas (414) 80 x 80 cm

private collection
illustrated on page 39

27. IMAGE OF FEDERICO GARCIA
LORCA 1978

Oil on canvas (416) 80 x 80 cms

exhibited
Galeria Maeght, Barcelona 1978:
Kreisler-Dos, Madrid 1979
Fundacion Rodriguez-Acosta, Granada
 1979
New York State Museum 1981
Boston College, Mass. 1982
Westfield College, Mass. 1982
Palais des Beaux Arts, Charleroi 1982

private collection
illustrated on page 39

28. IMAGE OF FEDERICO GARCIA
LORCA 1978-86

Oil on canvas (419) 146 x 114cms

exhibited
Galeria Maeght, Barcelona 1978:
Kreisler-Dos, Madrid 1979
Fundacion Rodriguez-Acosta, Granada
 1979
New York State Museum 1981
Boston College, 1982 Mass.
Westfield College, Mass. 1982
Palais des Beaux Arts, Charleroi 1982

collection
Fondation Maeght, St Paul, France
illustrated on page 40

29. IMAGE OF FEDERICO GARCIA
LORCA 1978

Oil on canvas (420) 146 x 114cms

exhibited
Galeria Maeght, Barcelona 1978:
Kreisler-Dos, Madrid 1979
Fundacion Rodriguez-Acosta, Granada
 1979
New York State Museum 1981
Boston College, Mass. 1982
Westfield College, Mass. 1982
Palais des Beaux Arts, Charleroi 1982

private collection
illustrated on page 42

30. SIX STUDIES TOWARD AN
IMAGE OF FEDERICO GARCIA
LORCA 1977

watercolour on paper
(w345) 39 x 39 cm
(w346) 39 x 39 cm
(w347) 39 x 35 cm
(w397) 39 x 35 cm
(w401) 39 x 39 cm
(w415) 39 x 39 cm

exhibited
Galeria Maeght, Barcelona 1978
Kreisler-Dos, Madrid 1979
Fundacion Rodriguez-Acosta, Granada
  1979
New York State Museum, 1981
Boston College, Mass. 1982
Westfield College, Mass. 1982
Palais des Beaux-Arts, Charleroi 1982

private collection
illustrated on page 41

31. IMAGE OF PICASSO 1983

Oil on canvas (489) 80 x 80 cms

exhibited
Musée Picasso, Antibes 1984

collection
Musée Picasso, Antibes
illustrated on page 45 and on back cover

32. IMAGE OF PICASSO 1983

Oil on canvas (490) 100 x 100 cms

exhibited
Galerie Municipale des Ponchettes,
  Nice 1985

private collection
illustrated on page 48

33. IMAGE OF PICASSO 1983

Oil on canvas (492) 100 x 100 cms

private collection
illustrated on page 46

34. IMAGE OF PICASSO 1983-87

Oil on canvas (548) 80 x 70 cms

private collection
illustrated on page 47

35. STUDIES TOWARD AN IMAGE
  OF PICASSO 1983 Triptych (w719)

Watercolour and crayon on paper
each 55 x 46 cms

exhibited
Musée Picasso, Antibes 1984 —

collection
Musée Picasso, Antibes
illustrated on page 44

36. IMAGE OF SAMUEL BECKETT
  1979-85

Oil on canvas (431) 70 x 70 cm

private collection
illustrated on page 53

37. IMAGE OF SAMUEL BECKETT
  1979

Oil on canvas (442) 80 x 80 cms

exhibited
Rosc '80, Dublin 1980
New York State Museum, 1981
Boston College, Mass. 1982
Westfield College, Mass. 1982
Palais des Beaux Arts, Charleroi 1982

private collection
illustrated on page 54

38. IMAGE OF SAMUEL BECKETT
  1980

Oil on canvas (451) 80 x 80 cms

exhibited
Rosc '80, Dublin 1980
New York State Museum, 1981
Boston College, Mass. 1982
Westfield College, Mass. 1982

Palais des Beaux Arts, Charleroi 1982

private collection
illustrated on page 55

39. IMAGE OF SAMUEL BECKETT
1982

Oil on canvas (473) 70 x 70 cms

private collection
illustrated on page 56

40. IMAGE OF SAMUEL BECKETT
1982

Oil on canvas (475) 73 x 73 cms

private collection
illustrated on page 60

41. IMAGE OF SAMUEL BECKETT
1987

Oil on canvas (544) 70 x 70 cms

private collection
illustrated on page 57

42. IMAGE OF SAMUEL BECKETT
1987

Oil on canvas (546) 65 x 50 cms

private collection
illustrated on page 59

43. IMAGE OF SAMUEL BECKETT
1987

Oil on canvas (547) 93 x 73 cms

private collection
illustrated on page 58 and on front
  cover (detail)

44. SIX STUDIES TOWARD AN
IMAGE OF SAMUEL BECKETT
1980

charcoal on paper
(c566) 76 x 56 cm
(c567) 76 x 56 cm
(c568) 76 x 56 cm
(c569) 76 x 56 cm
(c570) 76 x 56 cm
(c573) 76 x 56 cm

private collection
illustrated on page 61

45. IMAGE OF FRANCIS BACON
1979-86

Oil on canvas (436) 80 x 80 cms

originally exhibited
Rosc '80 Dublin 1980
New York State Museum, 1981
Boston College, Mass. 1982
Westfield College, Mass. 1982
Palais des Beaux Arts, Charleroi 1982

private collection
illustrated on pages 68 and 69

46. IMAGE OF FRANCIS BACON
1979

Oil on canvas (438) 80 x 80 cms

exhibited
Rosc '80 Dublin 1980
New York State Museum, 1981
Boston College, Mass. 1982
Westfield College, Mass. 1982
Palais des Beaux Arts, Charleroi 1982

private collection
illustrated on page 65

47. IMAGE OF FRANCIS BACON
1979-86

Oil on canvas (441) 80 x 80 cms

private collection
illustrated on page 67

48. IMAGE OF FRANCIS BACON
1985

Oil on canvas (536) 70 x 70 cms

private collection
illustrated on page 71

49. IMAGE OF FRANCIS BACON
1985

Oil on canvas (537) 100 x 100 cms

private collection, Chicago
illustrated on page 72

50. STUDIES TOWARD AN IMAGE
OF FRANCIS BACON 1982 Diptych
(w673)

watercolour and crayon on paper
each 61 x 46 cm

private collection
illustrated on page 64

51. STUDIES TOWARD AN IMAGE
OF FRANCIS BACON 1982 Diptych
(w674)

watercolour and crayon on paper
each 61 x 46 cm

private collection
illustrated on page 64

52. TWO STUDIES TOWARD AN
IMAGE OF FRANCIS BACON 1980

Watercolour and crayon on paper
(w510) 61 x 46 cm
(w524) 61 x 46 cm

private collection
illustrated on pages 66 and 70

ONE MAN EXHIBITIONS

Gimpel fils, London: 1947, 1949,
  1951, 1955, 1956, 1957, 1959,
  1961, 1968, 1971, 1974, 1978, 1983
Leicester Galleries, London 1948
Waddington Gallery, Dublin 1951
Venice Biennale, Irish pavilion 1956
Esther Robles Gallery, Los Angeles
  1960
Galerie Lienhard, Zurich 1961
Dawson Gallery, Dublin: 1962, 1966,
  1969, 1971, 1973, 1974, 1975
Municipal Gallery of Modern Art,
  Dublin (Retrospective) 1966, 1978
Ulster Museum, Belfast
  (Retrospective) 1967, 1987
Gimpel-Hanover Galerie, Zurich:
  1969, 1978
O.U.P., London 1970
Gimpel-Weitzenhoffer, New York:
  1971, 1978, 1983
McClelland Gallery, Belfast 1973
Fondation Maeght, St Paul de Vence
  1973
Galleria la Bussola, Turin 1974
Galerie La Demeure, Paris 1976
Arts Council Belfast: 1976, 1978
Municipal Gallery of Modern Art,
  Cork 1976
Musée d'Art Moderne de la Ville de
  Paris: 1976
Edinburgh Festival (Demarco Gallery)
  1977
Galleria San Marco, Genoa 1977
Waddington Galleries, Montreal and
  Toronto 1978
Galerie Maeght, Barcelona 1978
Galeria Kreisler-Dos, Madrid
  1978-1979
Fundacion Rodriguez-Acosta Granada
  1979
Galerie Jeanne Bucher, Paris: 1979,
  1982
Taylor Galleries, Dublin: 1981, 1985,
  1986
New York State Museum: 1981
Art 13, Basel (Galerie Börjeson) 1982
Boston College, Mass. 1982
Westbury College, Mass. 1982

Palais des Beaux Arts, Charleroi 1982
Galerie Gimpel Hanover Emmerich,
  Zurich 1983
Chicago International Expo. (Galerie
  Brownstone) 1986
Arts Council of Ireland, G.H.S.,
  Dublin 1987
Westpac Gallery, under aegis of
National Gallery of Victoria,
  Melbourne 1988

PUBLIC COLLECTIONS

Albright Knox Art Gallery, Buffalo
Arts Council of Ireland collection,
  Dublin
Arts Council of Great Britain
  collection, London
Bank of Ireland collection
Bord Fáilte Eireann collection, Dublin
Carnegie Institute, Pittsburg
Chicago Arts Club, Chicago
City Art Gallery, Leeds
City Art Gallery, Rugby
City Art Gallery, Waterford
Colombus Museum of Art, Ohio
Contemporary Art Society, London
Córas Trachtala collection, Dublin
Detroit Institute of Art, Detroit
Etat Francais, Service de la Création
  Artistique, Paris
Fondation Maeght, St Paul
Fort Worth Art Center, Texas
Foundation of Brazil Museum, Bahia
Graves Art Gallery, Sheffield
Gulbenkian Museum, Lisbon
Guggenheim Museum, New York
Hugh Lane Municipal Gallery of
  Modern Art, Dublin
International Collection, Abbot
  Laboratories, Chicago
International Hallmark award
  collection, New York
Joseph H. Hirshhorn Museum &
  Sculpture Garden, Washington
Kilkenny Art Gallery, Kilkenny
Kunsthaus, Zurich
La Prealpina SPA, Milan
McCrory Corporation, New York
Moravian Gallery, Brno
Municipal Gallery, Darlington
Municipal Gallery, Swindon
Musée d'Art Moderne de la Ville de
  Paris, Paris
Musée de Nantes
Musée Picasso, Antibes
National Gallery, New Delhi
National Gallery, Dublin
Nelson Art Gallery, New Zealand
New York State Museum
Pembroke College collection, Oxford

San Diego Museum of Art, California
D. & A. Smart Art Collection,
 University of Chicago
Tate Gallery, London
Trinity College collection, Dublin
Uffizi Gallery, Florence
Ulster Museum, Belfast
University of California, Berkeley
Victoria and Albert Museum, London

BIBLIOGRAPHY

BOOKS ILLUSTRATED BY LOUIS LE
BROCQUY

Austin Clarke, *Poetry in Modern
Ireland*, Cultural Relations
Committee, Dublin 1951
J.J. Campbell, *Irish Folk and Fairy
Tales*, Batsford, London 1955
Thomas Kinsella, *The Táin*, Dolmen
Press Dublin 1969, 1980, 1981,
1985. O.U.P. London, New York
1970, 1972, 1974, 1975, 1977,
1979, 1985, Heimeran Verlag,
Munich 1976. Dresden 1977
Desmond O'Grady, *The Gododdin*,
Dolmen Press, Dublin 1977
J. M. Synge, *The Playboy of the
Western World*, Imprint Society,
Mass. 1970
Seamus Heaney, *Ugolino*, Andrew
Carpenter, Dublin 1979
Eight Irish Writers., Collotype
lithographs with text. Ed: Andrew
Carpenter, Dublin 1981
James Joyce, *Dubliners*, Dolmen
 Press, Distributed Eason & Son,
 Dublin 1986

MONOGRAPH

Dorothy Walker, John Russell, *Louis
le Brocquy*, Ward River Press,
Dublin 1981
Hodder & Stoughton, London 1982

BOOKS ILLUSTRATING WORK

John Russell, *From Sickert to 1948*,
 Lund Humphreys, London 1948
Herbert Read, *Contemporary British
Art*, Penguin Books, London 1951
Herbert Read, *A Concise History of
Painting*, Thames & Hudson,
London 1959
50 Ans d'Art Moderne, Editions de la
 Connaissance S.A., Brussels 1959
Herbert Read, *Art since 1945*,
 Thames & Hudson, London 1959
F.D. Getlein, *Christianity in Modern
Art*, Bruce Publishing Co.,
 Milwaukee 1961
Herbert Read, *A letter to a Young
Painter*, Thames & Hudson, London,
1962
Brendan the Navigator., P.J. Carroll &
Co., Dublin 1964
Designers in Britain 6., Andre
Deutsch, London 1964
James White, *Tapisseries et Peintures
de Louis le Brocquy*, Revue
Francaise, Paris 1965
Basil Goulding, *Painting and
Sculpture of Today*, Hely Thom Ltd.
Dublin 1965
P. Wildbur, *A Handbook of
International Design*, Zwemmer,
London 1966
Variationen, Stadtische Kunsthalle,
Recklinghausen 1966
Bruce Arnold, *A Concise History of
Irish Art*, Thames & Hudson,
London 1969
Designers in Britain 7, Andre
Deutsch, London 1971
*La Fondation Marguerite et Aime
Maeght*., Maeght Editeur, Paris 1974
James Burns, *Leaving Certificate Art
History and Appreciation*, School
and College Services Ltd., Dublin
1976
Henry J. Sharpe, *Art History and
Appreciation*, Gill and Macmillan.,
Dublin 1976
Hugh MacDiarmid, *Frederick May*,
Woodtown Publications, Dublin
1976
Art Actuel, Skira Annuel, 1977
Peter Wilbur, *International
Trademark Design*, Barrie and
Jenkins, London 1979
L'Univers d'Aimé Maeght, Maison de
la Culture, Rennes, France 1979
Gomez Montero, *Entierro de Garcia
Lorca*, Granada 1979 (Cover)
The Council House, Peremeter Press,
Inc., U.S.A. 1980
A Vision, W.B. Yeats., Fayard, Paris,
1979 (Cover)
Modern Masters, Brahammar and
Garmer. Per-Olov Borjeson, Malmo
1980

Explorations, W.B. Yeats.
C.E.R.I.U.L., Lille 1981 (cover)
*Jacques Dupin, L'Espace Autrement
Dit*, Galilée, Paris 1982
Roderic Knowles, *Contemporary
Irish Art*, Wolfhound Press, Dublin
1982
Who's Who in Graphic Art, Amstutz
and Herdeg, Zurich 1982
Claude Esteban, *Traces, Figures,
Traversées*, Galilée, Paris 1985
Noel Kissane, *The Irish Face*, the
National Library of Ireland 1986
James Joyce. International
symposium, Copenhagen 1986.
Liam Miller, *Dolmen Book of Irish
Stamps*, Dolmen Press, Dublin 1987
Fondation Vincent Van Gogh, Arles
1987
L. Thorn Petit, *Portraits d'Artistes,
tome II*, RTL Edition, Luxembourg
1987
O'Riada Retrospective, Ed: Noel
Pearson, Dublin 1987

BOOKS WITHOUT ILLUSTRATION

Werner Haftmann, *Painting in the
Twentieth Century*, Lund
Humphreys, London 1961
Serge Faucherau, *Kinsella and le
Brocquy*, Critique, Paris 1970
Claude Esteban, *Traces, Figures,
Traversées*, Galilée, Paris 1985
Le Robert, *Dictionnaire Universelle
de la Peinture*, Paris 1986

REVIEWS ILLUSTRATING WORK

Earnán O Malley, *Louis le Brocquy*,
Horizon, London 1946
Spotlight on Dublin, Vogue, New
York 9 1946
Maurice Collis, *Louis le Brocquy*,
France Libre, London 1 1947
Home Brew. Time Magazine, New
York 10 3 1947
Maurice Collis, *Louis le Brocquy*,
Penguin Parade, London 1948
Guy Dornaud, *La Jeune Peinture
Britannique*, Franc Tireur, Paris 25 1
1948

Nevile Wallis, *Brave Ventures*,
Observer, London 29 1 1950
Mary Wallace, *The Art of Tapestry*,
Far and Wide, London, 2 1950
Young and Self-taught, Providence
Sunday Journal, USA 12 3 1950
James White, *Louis le Brocquy*,
Envoy, Dublin 5 1950
Louis le Brocquy Arts News and
Review, London, 6 1951
Eric Newton, *Round the London Art
Galleries*. The Listener, London 14 6
1951
Emily Grenauer, *The Cover Painting*.
What's New, Chicago, 3 1952
*Rejection of Art Work Criticised.
Irish Times*, Dublin 1 3 1952
Tapestry by Louis le Brocquy.
Ireland. Department of External
Affairs, Dublin 18 3 1952
Les Galeries, Lettres Francaises, Paris
13 11 1952
Les Galeries, Lettres Francaise, Paris
20 11 1952
Studio Flat. House & Garden,
London, 7 1953
*La 3a Mostra Internazionale di Bianco
e Nero*. Rivista Tecnica Lugano, 3
1954
Painter's Fabrics. Architectural
Review , London, 7 1954
*Le Brocquy Designs, Pattern in
Contrast*. Ambassador No. 10
London 1955
Michael Middleton, *Louis le Brocquy*.
Art News & Review, London, 2
1955
W.J. Strachen, *Contemporary
Tapestries from France and Britain*,
Studio, London, 12 1955
E.von Glasersfelt, *Die 28 Biennale in
Venedig*, Standpunkt, Meran, Italy
1956
Robert Melville, *Exhibitions*,
Architectural Review, London, 4
1955
Artist's Success in Venice. Sunday
Press, Dublin 19 8 1956
J.E. Cirlot, *Revista de Arte*, Goya No.
10, Madrid 1956
*Design at Source. Exhibition of le
Brocquy Designs*. Ambassador,

London 9 1956
People are Talking About. Vogue,
London, 3 1957
Robert Melville. Architectural Review,
London, 6 1957
Lawrence Alloway, *Introduction*,
Kunstkring, Rotterdam 1957
Trust Buys Painting. Dublin Evening
Press, Dublin 28 8 1958
Michael Shepherd, *The Light of
Space*, Art News & Review, London,
11 1959
T. McGreevy, *Art Contemporain en
Irlande*, Prisme des Arts No. 18,
Paris 1959
Basil Goulding, *One Man's Meat*, Arts
Council, Dublin 11 1961
F. Rogon, *Huit Jours a Londres*,
Cimaise, Paris, 7 1961
Art. What's on in London, London
29 9 1961
Study of Head. House & Garden,
London, 2 1962
*Le Brocquy Painting for Dublin
Gallery*. Irish Times, Dublin 17 8
1962
R. Penrose and H. Read, *Reflections
on Contemporary European
Painting*, Marzotto Valdagno 1962
A Memorable Tapestry. J.W. Irish
Times, Dublin 5 6 1964
Mosaic Mural. Interior Design,
London, 1 1964
James White, *Tapisseries et Peintures
de Louis le Brocquy*
La Revue Francaise, Paris, 5 1965
Bruce Laughton, *Louis le Brocquy*.
Arts review, London 5 3 1966
John Fitzmaurice Mills, *Art Forum*.
Irish Times, Dublin 19 4 1966
John Montague, *Louis le Brocquy. A
Painter's Interior World*.
Hibernia, Dublin, December 1966
Anne Crookshank, *Ireland*. External
Affairs Bulletin 749, 13 1 1967
A. Magnien, *Carrossois d'adoption
Louis le Brocquy expose a Londres*.
Nice Matin, October 1968
The Táin. Editorial, Ireland of the
Welcomes, March/April 1969
A. Butler, *Emormous Range of le
Brocquy*. Evening Press, Dublin, 16

9 1969

Graphics by le Brocquy. Irish Times, 16 9 1969

B. Wright, *Louis le Brocquy.* Arts review, 9 9 1971

Jean-Marie Benoist, *Louis le Brocquy.* L'Art Vivant, March 1973

L'Exposition le Brocquy; angoisse et silence. A.S. Nice Matin, 10 3 1973

Dorothy Walker, *Le Brocquy at the Fondation Maeght,* Hibernia, 13 4 1973

Brian Fallon, *Le Brocquy's Táin Tapestries.* Irish Times, 10 5 1973

Dorothy Walker, *Tapestries and Graphics.* Hibernia, 25 5 1973

John Montague, *'Primal scream — the late le Brocquy'.* The Arts in Ireland, Vol. II, No. 1, 1973.

Pierre Rouve, *Le Brocquy.* Arts Review, London, 4 9 1974

Dorothy Walker, Art From Three Cities. Hibernia, 12 12 1975

Caroline Tisdall, Cork Trip. The Guardian, 16 12 1975

Dorothy Walker, *The word and the image.* Ireland Today 881, 13 2 1976,

Striking Exhibition. Cork Examiner, 17 3 1976

Anne Yeats, *Yeats aux cent portraits au Musée d'Art Moderne.* Quotidien de Paris, 7 11 1976

Anne Cremin, *In Search of Yeats.* Irish Times, 10 11 1976

Germano Beringheli, *Il ritratto di uno scrittore.* Il Laroro, Genoa, 22 11 1977

Il volto di Joyce, Il Secolo XIX, Genoa, 19 11 1977

Louis le Brocquy. Corriere Mercantile, Genoa, 22 11 1977

John Montague, *The Faces of Yeats.* Etudes Irlandaises, December 1977.

Joyce vu par le Brocquy. Art Vivant, Chroniques, Paris, March 1978

Louise Collis, *Louis le Brocquy at Gimpel Fils.* Arts Review London, 12 5 1978

Roger Berthoud, *All in the Head.* The Times, London, 15 3 1978

Louise Collis, *Art and Artist,* London

May 1978

John Montague, *Jaweyes.* Art International, XII/6, 1978

Brian Lynch, *Still Life.* Hibernia, 13 7 1978

Blaithain O Ciobhain, *Impressions.* Irish Press, 7 7 1978

Gallery Previews in New York. Pictures on Exhibit, New York, October 1978

John Russell, *Dublin's Own Image in le Brocquy's Joyce.* The New York Daily Metro, 22 9 1978

Le Brocquy y Van Velde, en Maeght. Destino, Barcelona, 26 9 1978

Le Brocquy, analista de un solo nostro. Diario de Barcelona, 28 9 1978

Gomez Montero, *Ochenia y ocho estudios para una figura de Garcia Lorca.* Ideal, Granada, 21 11 1978

88 Estudios para una figura de Federico. Hoja del Lunes, Granada, 17 11 1978

Ciarán Mac Gonigal, *Louis le Brocquy.* Ireland Today 940, 1 12 1978.

Department of Foreign Affairs, *Dublin Los blancos laberintos: le Brocquy vea Lorca.* El Imparcial, Madrid, 30 12 1978

John Montague, *Jaweyes.* The Crane Bag, Vol. 2, No. 1 & 2, Dublin 1978

P.R. Shepherd, *Consciousness-raising.* Onion, Toronto, February 1979

Studies for an image of Lorca. London Magazine, March 1979

R.G. Montero, *La Obra de Louis le Brocquy.* Calle Elvira, Granada, June 1979

Exposiciones. Cambino 16, Madrid, 1 1 1979

Maïten Bouisset, *Les Portraits de Louis le Brocquy.* Le Matin, Paris, 25 12 1979

La memoire celte de Louis le Brocquy. Conaissance des Arts, December 1979

Gilles Plazy, *Louis le Brocquy à la Galerie Jeanne Bucher, têtes Magiques.* Quotidien de Paris, 1 1 1980

Kate Robinson, Shocks, Delights and Bad Lighting. Hibernia, Dublin, 31 7 1980

Kate Robinson, *What Rosc '80 Means.* Hibernia, Dublin, 25 7 1980

Rosc '80. Arts and Studies, Irish Times, July 1980 — photographic survey.

Rosc '80. Business and Finance, Dublin 21 8 1980

Emmanuel Kehoe, *Tete a Tete,.* Sunday Press, Dublin 20 7 1980

Paul Overy. *Dublin: Rosc '80.* Flash Art, Milan, international edition, October 1980

G. Boudaille. *Rosc a Dublin.* L'Oeil, September 1980

Anne Cremin, *Louis le Brocquy.* Image, Ocotober 1980

Dorothy Walker, Louis le Brocquy. The Conoisseur, London 1981

Drusilla Beyfus, *"Spotlight".* Vogue, London, February 1981

John Russell, *Louis le Brocquy and the Celtic Head.* New York Times, 6 11 1981

Illustrated catalogue of acquisitions 1978-1980. The Tate Gallery, London 1981

James White, *Essence of a Painter.* Irish Times, November 1981

Aidan Dunne, *Le Brocquy: archaeologist of the spirit.* "In Dublin Magazine", December 1981

Louis le Brocquy. The Sunday Tribune magazine. 13 December 1981

Jean-Marie Tasset, *Louis le Brocquy: la Tete des Autres.* Figaro 13 October 1982

James Joyce Centenary issue. Etudes Irlandaises, Lille 1982 (cover)

Maïten Bouisset *Louis le Brocquy* Goya, revista de Arte, Madrid 1982

Jacques Dupin, *Louis le Brocquy* Mathieu Benezet, *Voici que les peintres....*

Serge Fauchereau, *la peinture de Louis le Brocquy.* Digraphe No. 27, Juin 1982

Richard Kearney, *Joyce and le Brocquy: Art as Otherness.* The

Crane Bag Vol. 6, No. 1 1982

Freddy de Vree, *Louis le Brocquy*. N.W.T. December 1984

Ann Cremin *Louis le Brocquy*. S & P, Dublin December 1984

Dorothy Walker, Contemporary Irish Tapestry. Irish Arts Review summer 1984

Dorothy Walker, *Louis le Brocquy: The New Work*. Irish Arts Review Vo. 2, No. 7, Spring 1985

Anne Cremin, *Friend Game*. Interview with Samuel Beckett. Art News, New York, May 1985

Mary Dowey, *The Head Master*. Image November 1986

REVIEWS WITHOUT ILLUSTRATION

Paintings and Sculpture. Irish Times, Dublin 14 12 1942

Stephen Rynne. *Art Alive*. The Leader, Dublin 25 9 1943

Michael MacLiammoir. *I.E.L.A.* The Bell, Dublin 10 1945

Irish Artists. New York Herald Tribune, New York 4 3 1947

The Irish. New Yorker, New York 15 3 1947

Maurice Collis. *le Brocquy* Observer, London 25 5 1947 *The Painter from Dublin*. Harpers Bazaar, London 5 1947

Mr Le Brocquy's Water Colours. The Times, London 26 5 1947

M.H.Middleton. *Art*. Spectator, London 30 5 1947

Maurice Collis. *Art*. Time & Tide, London 7 6 1947

La Jeune Peinture Anglaise. Rayonnement des Beaux Arts, Paris 15 2 1948

Maurice Collis. *Natural Drawing versus Pattern*. Time & Tide, London 19 6 1948

Mr Le Brocquy's Pictures. The Times, London 22 6 1948

Mr Louis Le Brocquy. The Times, London 22 9 1948

David Silvester. *Louis Le Brocquy*. Art News & Reviews, London 22 9 1949

Round the Galleries. New Statesman, London 22 9 1949

John Berger. *Two British Painters*.

New Statesman, London 16 6 1951

Eric Newton. *Two Contemporary Painters*. Time & Tide, London 16 6 1951

John Berger. *Distinguished Humility*. Art News, London 16 6 1951

Le Brocquy's Art is Varied. Irish Press, Dublin 7 12 1951

What is it all about. A.H.R. Evening Herald Dublin 11 12 1951

John Ryan. *The Louis Le Brocquy Exhibition,* Our Nation, Dublin 1

1952 Rejection of Art Works Criticised. Irish Times, Dublin 29 2 1952

Gallery Refuses Gift of £420 Painting. Sunday Express, London 2 3 1952

At Cross Purposes. Leading artical. Evening Mail, Dublin 6 3 1952

Rejection of Picture. IELA. Irish Times, Dublin 8 3 1952

Edward Sheehy. *Art Notes*. Dublin Magazine, Dublin 1952

Louis le Brocquy. Irish Times, Dublin 21 8 1954

Stephen Bone. *Louis le Brocquy*, The Guardian, Manchester 4 2 1955

Nevile Wallis. *Varied Talents*. Observer, London 6 2 1955

Art. Spectator, London 18 2 1955

Mr Le Brocquy's New Paintings. The Times, London 22 2 1955

R Spira. *Le Brocquy: Ein Irischer Maler*. Der Standpunkt, Meran, 1955

James White. *Louis le Brocquy*. Catalogue. Biennale, Venice, 6 1956

Painting Rejected by Dublin Wins Venice Prize. Irish Pres, Dublin 6 1956

A Strange Painter. The Times, London 28 2 1957

Pierre Rouve. *Post Brutism*. Art News & Reviews, London 2 3 1957

John Golding. *Extrovert and Introvert,* New Statesman, London 9 3 1957

John Russell. *Explorers*. Sunday Times, London 10 3 1957

Nevile Wallis. *Changing Modes*. Observer, London 10 3 1957

Stephen Bone. *Two Painters*. The Guardian. Manchester 10 3 1957

Jonge Engelse Schilders. Algemeen Handelsplad, Amsterdam 26 3 1958

Neue Malerie aus England. Dusseldorfer Nachuchten, Dusseldorf 2 7 1958

Young British Painters. St Gallen Tagblatt, St. Gallen 31 5 1958

Enigmatic Studies in White. The Times, London 3 11 1959

Shadows on a White Ground. Frederick Laws. The Guardian. Manchester 11 11 1959

James White. *Le Brocquy Exibition in London*. Irish Times, Dublin 13 11 1959

John Russell. *The Loss of Lane*. Sunday Times, London 15 11 1959

Nevile Wallis. *The Irish Question*. Observer, London 15 11 1959

Tate Gallery Report, 1958-59. London 1959

Tate Gallery Report, 1959-60, London 1960

Louis le Brocquy. Neue Zurcher Zeitung, Zurich 13 1 1961

Skilful Variations of Paint Texture. J.M.N. Yorkshire Post, Leeds 13 9 1961

Mr Le Brocquy's Sensuous Paintings. The Times, London 14 9 1961

Nevile Wallis. *Adler and le Brocquy*. Observer, London 17 9 1961

Michael Shepherd. *Louis le Brocquy*. Art News & Review, London 23 9 1961 Eric Newton. *A Bang and a Whisper*. The Guardian. Manchester 21 9 1961

John Russell. *Not Meant to be Admired*. Sunday Times, London 24 9 1961

Painter who flirts with Poetry. The Scotsman, Edinburgh 2 10 1961

James White. *Louis le Brocquy Exibits Recent Paintings*. Irish Times, Dublin 21 6 1962

Rewarding Show of Paintings. P.H.G. Irish Independant, Dublin 22 6 1962

Marion Burleigh. *Exciting le Brocquy Exibition*. Irish Press, Dublin 23 6 1962

Municipal Gallery given new Work. Irish Independant, Dublin 18 8 1962

Mode med Britisk Kunst. Tof. Vestkysten, Denmark 14 9 1962

Ny Britisk Kunst. Ejner Johansson. Information, Copenhagen 8 1 1963

St Brendan Tapestry. Irish Times, Dublin 5 6 1964

Miriam Hederman. *Louis le Brocquy*. Irish Press, Dublin 8 3 1965

Enfant Terrible. News Letter, Belfast 3 3 1966

A Case of Head or Torso. The Times, London 5 3 1966
Triple Home. Evening Standard, London 9 3 1966
Art. What's On. London 11 3 1966
David Thompson. Art. Sunday Times, London 13 3 1966
Edwin Mullins. Art. Sunday Telegraph, London 13 3 1966
Le Brocquy retrospective. B.P.F. Irish Times, Dublin, 11 11 1966
A. Butler. Emotion with Discipline. Evening Press, Dublin, November 1966
I Saw a Ship A-Sailing. The Tablet, 21 1 1967
Bruce Arnold. The Style of Louis le Brocquy. Sunday Independant, 6 9 1968
Louis le Brocquy H.C., Werk. Winterhur, Switzerland, March 1969
Frissons Fur Die Gute Gesellschaft. Tages Anzeiger. Zurich 25 1 1969
Erika Billeter. Louis le Brocquy in der Galerie Gimpel & Hanover. Zurich 16 1 1969
Dorothy Walker. The Táin Tapestry. Irish Times, Dublin 17 9 1970
Brian Fallon. Le Brocquy. Irish Times, Dublin 21 9 1971
Bruce Arnold. Louis Le Brocquy. Irish Independant 25 9 1971
Dorothy Walker. Rosc Round-up. Hibernia 19 11 1971
Michel Gaudet. Louis le Brocquy a la la Fondation Maeght. Patriote, March 1973
Max Wykes-Joyce. Around European Galleries. International Herald Tribune, Paris, 5 9 1974
Brian Fallon. Le Brocquy Etchings at Dawson Gallery. Irish Times, 4 9 1974
Le Brocquy à la recherche de Yeats. G.B. Le Monde, Paris 10 11 1971
Pierre Mazars. Louis Le Brocquy dans la maniere de Pirandello. Le Figaro. Paris 26 9 1976
A la Recherche de W.B. Yeats. Art Vivant, Chroniques, Paris. December 1976
Anne Yeats. Faces of my Father. Irish Times, December 1976
Edward Gage. Lighting up the face of pre-history. The Scotsman. Edinburugh, 29 8 1977
Felice Ballero. Le Brocquy spiega

Joyce. Gazzetta del Lunedi Genoa 14 11 1977
Louis le Brocquy malt Joyce. neue Zurcher Zeitung 10 2 1978
Entschwundenes Sujet. Tages-Anzeiger Zurich31 1 1978
Max Wykes-Joyce. Louis le Brocquy. International Herald Tribune. Paris 1 4 1978
Annabel Terry Engel. Louis le Brocquy. Studies towards an image of James Joyce. Arts Review. London 17 3 1978

Louis le Brocquy. Art Vivant, Chroniques, Paris, May 1978
Lettre de New York. Vie des Arts. No 94 Paris 5 5 1979
Louis le Brocquy. "une archeologie de l'esprit" J.M.T. Nice Matin, 9 2 1979
Ciaran Carty. Eggs in the Sand. Sunday Independant, 7 10 1979
Louis le Brocquy en Maeght. La Vanguardia, Barcelona 3 11 1978
Andre Fermigier. Les Jeux de Tetes de le Brocquy. Le Monde. Paris 22 12 1979
Georges Raillard. Louis le Brocquy. La Quinzaine Litteraire. Paris 16 12 1979
Michel Nuridsany. L'Art magique de le Brocquy. Le Figaro. Paris 21 12 1979
Michael Gibson. Louis le Brocquy. International Herald Tribune. 15 12 1979
Jorge Glusberg. Rosc '80. Artinf., Buenos Aires, November-December 1980
Dorothy Walker. Rosc '80. Ireland Today. September 1980
Raoul-Jean Moulin. Poesie de la vision '80. L'Humanité. Paris 7 10 1980
Al festival col reverendo. Il Giarnale Nuovo, Milan, 26 9 1980
Anne Dagbert. Rosc '80. Art Press. Paris. October 1980
Paddy Agnew. The Irish Artists in Rosc '80. Magill. Dublin June 1980
More Than One. Vogue, Feburary 1981
John Russell. Louis le Brocquy. New York Times 6 1 81

Bruce Arnold. The Measure of Consent. 'Books Ireland'', Dublin. June 1982
Louis le Brocquy Book Review. Irish Weekly 20 Dec 1981
Michael Gibson. Shakespearean 'Head-Images' by le Brocquy. International Herald Tribune. October 9-10 1982
Shakespeares imaginares Gesicht. Zurichsee-Seitung 20 Jan 1983
John Russell. Louis le Brocquy. New York Times 14 Oct 1983
Jerry Tallmer. To Draw or Not to Draw Shakespeare. New York Post 15 Oct 1983
Aidan Dunne. Ebb Tide le Brocquy. The Sunday Press. Dublin March 31 1985
James White. Portrait of the Artist at 70. Irish Times. Nov 8 1986
Aidan Dunne. Portrait of the Artist as an old man. Sunday Press, Dublin 9 1986

EXHIBITION CATALOGUES
ILLUSTRATING WORKS

Denys Sutton, Louis le Brocquy, Gimpel Fils, London 1947
Mostra dei Premiati alla XXVIII Biennale di Venezia 1956 Cinquante Ans d'Art Moderne, Exposition International de Bruxelles 1958
Louis le Brocquy Gimpel Fils London 1959
Robert Melville, Louis le Brocquy Galerie Leinhard, Zurich 1961
Herbert Read, Louis le Brocquy. Gimpel Fils. London 1961
Louis le Brocquy, Dawson Gallery, Dublin 1962
Seven Tapestries 1948-1955. Dawson Gallery, 1966
Ulster Museum, Belfast 1967
Jacques Dupin, Le Brocquy Gimpel Fils, London 1966
Anne Crookshank, Jacques Dupin, A Retrospective Selection of Oil Paintings, Municipal Gallery, Dublin, 1966, Ulster Museum Belfast 1967
Zauber des Lichtes. Stadtische Kunsthalle, Recklinghausan 1967
L'Art Vivant,1965-1968 Fondation Maeght, St Paul 1968
Louis le Brocquy Gimpel Fils,

London, Zurich 1968.
Louis le Brocquy Gimpel Weitzenhoffer, New York 1971
Brian O'Doherty, Thomas Kinsella, *The Irish Imagination 1951-1971*
Louis le Brocquy Dawson Gallery, Dublin 1971
Claude Esteban, Jacques Dupin, Fondation Maeght, St Paul 1973
John Montague, *Louis le Brocquy*. Gimpel Fils, London; La Bussola, Turin, 1974
L. le Brocquy, J. Lassaigne, J. Montague *A la Recherche- de W.B. Yeats*, Musée d'Art Moderne de la Ville de Paris, 1976
John Montague, Louis le Brocquy, *Studies toward an Image of James Joyce* Gimpel Fils; Touring Genoa, Zurich, London, Belfast, Dublin, New York, Montreal, Toronto, 1977-1978
Claude Esteban, *88 Studies toward an image of Federico Garcia Lorca* Galeria Maeght, Barcelona 1978, Madrid, Granada 1979
Alan Bosquet, *Europe des Peintures* Issy Brachot, Brussels 1979
Michael Peppiatt, Louis le Brocquy, Galerie Jeanne Bucher,Paris 1979
Jacques Dupin, *Le Corps et les Peintures Actuels*, Ch.Musée, Cagnes-sur-Mer 1979
Cyril Barrett *Irish Art 1943-1973*. Cork 1980
Frances Ruane, *The Delighted Eye*, Arts Council of Ireland, London 1980
Anne Crookshank, *Rosc '80*, Dublin 1980
Dorothy Walker, *Catalogue of Works of Art*, Bank Of Ireland, Dublin 1980
Illustrated Catalogue of Acquisitions 1978-80, Tate Gallery, London
Anne Crookshank, *Louis le Brocquy and the Celtic Head Image,* New York State Museum 1981; Boston College, Mass, Westfield College Mass. 1982
Art 13'82 Internationale Kunstmesse, Basel 1982
Serge Fauchereau, Louis le Brocquy. Palais des Beaux Arts de Charleroi 1982
Frances Ruane, *Six Artists from Ireland*, Irish Arts Council, Dublin

1983, touring
Jacques Derrida, Michel Leiris, *Art Contre/Against Apartheid* U.N.E.S.C.O., Paris 1983
Brian Robertson, *English Contrasts, Peintres et Sculpteurs Anglais 1950-1960* Artcurial, Paris Sept-Nov 1984
Twentieth Century Irish Art A.I.B. Collection, D.Hyde Gallery, Dublin 1986

TEXTS AND INTERVIEWS

Pattern in Contrast: Hot, Dull — Cool, Bright. A colour impression by Louis le Brocquy. The Ambassador. No. 10 London. 1955
Thoughts on our Time and Jean Lurçat. Art 17, Royal College of Art, London 1956. Reprinted in 'Seven Tapestries 1948 — 1955'. Ulster Museum Belfast. December 1967
Harriet Cooke talks to Louis le Brocquy. Irish Times 25 5 1973
The Mystery of Fact review, Interviews with Francis Bacon: Introspect, Dublin, Dec 1975.

La Culture Gauloise Catalogue la Demeure, Paris, Sept. 1976
L'Oeuvre Unique, (Henri Michaux, Louis le Brocquy), Skira Annual 1977
Artist's Note, The Gododdin, D. O'Grady, Dolmen Press, Dublin 1977
A Painters Notes on Ambivalence. The Crane Bag, Vol. 1 No. 2 Dublin 1977
Jean-Marie Benoist, *Interview with Louis le Brocquy*. Hibernia 1 9 1977
Bernard Noel interviews Louis le Brocquy. Introspect. Dublin Dec 1977
Notes on Painting and Awareness. Corps-poésie-peinture. Actes du colloque reuni le 8, 9 et 10 Fevrier 1979 a la Faculté des Lettres de Nice; METAPHORES no. 5, Universite de Nice.

Reprinted in *Etudes Irlandaises, CERIUL Lille* Dec 1979.
Louis le Brocquy Dorothy Walker, Ward River Press, Dublin 1981;
Michael Peppiatt, *Interview with Louis le Brocquy*. Art International, Lugano, Oct 1979
Artist in Landscape. Interview Cara, Aer Lingus, Sept 1981
A Painter's Notes on his Irishness. The Recorder Vol. 42, The American Irish Historical Society, New York 1981. Reprinted in *Louis le Brocquy*, D. Walker. Ward River, Dublin 1981. Reprinted in *Irishness in a Changing Society*, Pierre Joannon, Colin Symth, London 1987
Quelques notes d'un peintre a propos de son Irlandité. Digraphe Messidon/Temps Actuels; Paris, June 1982.
M. Benezet, S Faucherau, J Ristat, *Conversation avec Louis le Brocquy*. Digraphe, Messidor/Temps Actuels, Paris, June 1982

FILMS

Interview with the Artist. Patrick Gallagher. Folio. R.T.E. Dec 1981
Portrait D'Artiste: L le Brocquy. L. Thorn-Petit. RTL 22/4/83
Louis le Brocquy, An Other Way of Knowing. A film portrait by Michael Garvey. R.T.E. 1986

DESIGNED BY RAYMOND KYNE DESIGN ASSOCIATES, DUBLIN.
TYPESET IN GARAMOND BY KEYSTROKES.
COLOUR SEPARATIONS BY PENTACOLOUR INTERNATIONAL LIMITED.
PRINTED IN IRELAND BY IRISH PRINTERS LIMITED,
ON HUNTSMAN SILK 170 GSM PAPER AND TRUCOTE 280 GSM ART BOARD